Berries Beautiful!

An All-Seasons Cookbook

For Lovers
of Strawberries
and Raspberries

by
Carol Kutzli Olson
B. Sc. (H.Ec.) in Foods and Nutrition

Berries Beautiful
by Carol Olson

First Printing — May, 1985

Copyright © 1985 by
Carol Olson Publishing
P.O. Box 3
Spy Hill, Saskatchewan S0A 3W0

Canadian Cataloguing in Publication Data
Olson, Carol, 1933-
Berries Beautiful

Includes index.
ISBN 0-919845-27-4

1. Cookery (Raspberries) 2. Cookery (Strawberries) I. Title.
TX813.B40447 1985   641.6'4711   C85-091270-9

Strawberry Sketches by
Jean Noethlich

Photography by
Patricia Holdsworth
Patricia Holdsworth Photography
Regina, Saskatchewan

Dishes page 16 courtesy of
Eaton's, Cornwall Centre, Regina, Sask.
Background Tiles courtesy of
Alpine Marble & Tile, Regina, Sask.

Design by Blair Fraser
Designed, Printed and Produced in Canada by
Centax of Canada
1048 Fleury Street
Regina, Saskatchewan, Canada   S4N 4W8

#105 - 4711 13 Street N.E.
Calgary, Alberta, Canada   T2E 6M3

Introduction

Strawberries and red raspberries are beautiful fruits that can be enjoyed in all seasons. They are unsurpassed as fresh fruit to eat plain or used in various recipes. Frozen berries can be substituted for fresh berries in many recipes. Other recipes are specifically designed for the use of frozen fruit. Jams and jellies have multiple uses.

They are also fruits that bring back special memories to many. Memories of trying to grow the plants, picking the berries or the pleasure of eating the fruit.

Most years my parents had two very long rows of strawberries at home in Ohio. In good years they provided strawberries for ourselves and the neighbors. There was the odd year when we didn't have strawberries, and it was then that we visited a U-pick farm.

After moving to Saskatchewan I found the growing of strawberries to be more difficult because of lack of plant hardiness and uncertain weather conditions. However; years of research and study have developed more vigorous plants and, with favorable weather, strawberries and red raspberries grown on the prairies are of excellent quality.

The U-pick system is used on our farm. I was familiar with this system in Ohio and I found the history of the development on the prairies interesting. Peter J. Peters, a former fruit specialist with Manitoba Department of Agriculture was generous in writing the history for this book and granted permission to use a portion of his poem **Ode To the Strawberry.**

"**A gourmet's dream, a meal's delight**
That tempts your taste with color bright
The strawberry makes lovers sing
Of all the fruits, it is the king.

So here's an ode to this rare treat
The fairest fruit there is to eat.
It fills most hearts with joy and glee
This beauty fruit, the strawberry."

The strawberry is called the King of the fruits, so surely the red raspberry must be the Queen.

Development of the U-Pick System

In the early 1960's the Manitoba Department of Agriculture began an experiment and demonstration designed to prove that commercial strawberry production in Western Canada was feasible. The provincial fruit specialist organized the Reynold's Strawberry Growers' Co-op to assist him in this venture. A 39-acre field bordered by the Whitemouth River was purchased. The objectives of the experiment were four-fold: (1) to choose suitable varieties; (2) to introduce new, mechanized growing practices, including straw mulching; (3) to use irrigation to maximize yields and frost control; (4) to market the crop at a profit.

The first three objectives were reached and in three years' time a clean, weed-free, well-strawed 10 acre field of strawberries with a good set of fruit was ready for picking. There was only one problem, the necessay labor force. An emergency call went out via T.V., radio and the press. People were advised that they could Pick-Your-Own strawberries at 25¢ a pound at Hadashville, and bring your own containers. The response was overwhelming. On the first day some 1000 people showed up at the strawberry field. Some came as early as six o'clock in the morning. By ten o'clock all the ripe berries were picked, weighed and paid for. Many people had to go home empty handed. The cooperative arranged for three picking days a week. By the end of the season some 75,000 pounds of berries had been sold, all by the U-Pick system. The returns proved profitable.

The Co-op continued this method of marketing in the following years. Within ten years a goodly number of strawberry enterprises sprang up in many parts of Manitoba. All of them eventually adopted the U-Pick system for their crop.

Over the years the U-Pick system has undergone many changes. Selling by weight has been replaced by selling by containers, such as gallon pails or 4-quart or 4-liter baskets. Parking facilities, restrooms, shaded lunch areas, and play areas for children make the U-Pick outing a pleasant holiday for customers. Provincial maps, showing the locations, names, and phone numbers of the many strawberry operations, are available. These are augmented by T.V., radio, and newspaper advertising. The U-Pick system that began as an emergency operation at Hadashville, has become the recognized system of strawberry marketing in Western Canada.

Table of Contents

 All recipes are given in both standard and metric measurements for your convenience. All have been tested in the standard measurements but have not been tested specifically with the metric conversions.

Care of Strawberries and Raspberries

The fresh fruit should be kept in a cool area but should not be wet. The berries should be washed just prior to use. Strawberries should be washed with caps or hulls on. The cap is removed when the strawberries are clean. The raspberries should be checked for any small particles. Any immature berries should be discarded. The clean berries should be dried on paper towels or at least drained in a colander.

Freezing

When freezing, one should consider the purpose for which the fruit will be used. The strawberries can be left whole or sliced. The berries can be packed in various-sized containers, 1 cup (250 mL) and 2 cups (500 mL) being the most popular. All containers should be well marked with name of fruit, date, quantity and type of pack. If jam or jelly is to be prepared with frozen fruit, the fruit should be packed in measured amounts for a specific recipe.

The use of sugar on the berries varies with the individual. Many freeze the berries without sugar. Others prefer adding ¾ cup (175 mL) sugar per quart (1 L) of fruit in a dry pack. The sugar and berries should be combined before packing in freezing containers. A syrup pack of 3 cups (750 mL) sugar per 1 quart (1 L) of water can be used for dessert berries. An unsweetened liquid pack of 1 tsp. (5 mL) ascorbic acid per 1 quart (1 L) of water can be used for color and flavor retention.

Most of our customers prefer the dry pack without sugar. We find frozen berries to be at their best if frozen shortly after picking.

Thawing

Frozen berries should be thawed in unopened containers, unless one is using a microwave. I prefer to empty a package into a suitable dish for microwave use. Set microwave on defrost for 3 to 4 minutes. Check berries and defrost another few minutes if necessary. Berries thawed in a microwave have excellent color and flavor retention and the liquid seems of a syrup consistency when packed without sugar. Generally berries should be thawed to the point where some ice crystals remain. However, if the fruit is being used in a jellied salad or dessert this would not apply.

Beverages
Soups

Berry-Wheat Germ Beverage

1 cup	milk, cold	250 mL
1	banana	1
3 tbsp.	wheat germ	50 mL
2 tbsp.	strawberry OR raspberry jam	25 mL

Combine all ingredients in blender. Blend until smooth.
SERVES: 2.

Strawberry or Raspberry Punch

12½ oz.	frozen orange juice	355 mL
12½ oz.	frozen lemonade	355 mL
14 oz.	crushed pineapple and juice	398 mL
4 cups	home-frozen strawberries or raspberries, partly thawed	1 L
	OR	
4 x 10 oz.	pkg. commercially frozen strawberries or raspberries, partly thawed	4 x 283 g
¼ cup	lemon or lime concentrate	50 mL
6 cups	ginger ale	2 x 750 mL
3 trays	ice cubes	3 trays

Shortly before serving, combine all ingredients. For a sweeter punch dissolve sugar in boiling water; add to punch.
SERVES: 50 punch cups.

BERRY QUICK FRUIT AND WINE:
Combine strawberries, seedless green grapes and sliced nectarines. Add wine and refrigerate several hours.

Berry-Yogurt Shake

¾ cup	fresh strawberries or raspberries	175 mL
2 tbsp.	honey	25 mL
1 cup	milk, cold	250 mL
1 cup	yogurt	250 mL

Purée berries in blender. Add remaining ingredients and blend until smooth.

NOTE: Seeds can be removed by forcing purée through a sieve if so desired.
SERVES: 2.

Strawberry Daiquiris

6 tbsp.	light rum	85 g
¼ cup	lime juice	50 mL
2 tbsp.	sugar	25 mL
2 cups	frozen whole strawberries, partly thawed	500 mL

Combine in a blender the rum, lime juice and sugar. Blend to dissolve sugar. Add partly thawed strawberries and blend until smooth.
SERVES: 2.

Strawberry Limeade

1 cup	sugar	250 mL
5 cups	cold water	1.25 L
1 cup	lime juice, fresh	250 mL
1 cup	puréed strawberries	250 mL

Combine sugar and 1 cup (250 mL) of water. Bring to a boil and boil 5 minutes. Cool. Add remaining cold water, lime juice and puréed strawberries. Serve chilled. Garnish with lime slices and mint leaves.
YIELDS: 1½ quarts (1.5 L). See photograph page 16.

Colada

2 cups	crushed pineapple and juice	500 mL
⅔ cup	yogurt	150 mL
¼ cup	coconut liqueur	50 mL
1 cup	fresh strawberries OR	250 mL
1 cup	whole frozen strawberries, partly thawed	250 mL

Place all ingredients in blender and blend until smooth. Add crushed ice and serve.
YIELDS: 3 cups (750 mL).

Two-Berry Shrub

2 cups	home-frozen raspberries, thawed, OR	500 mL
2 x 10 oz.	pkgs. commercially frozen raspberries, thawed	2 x 283 g
2 cups	home-frozen strawberries, thawed, OR	500 mL
2 x 10 oz.	pkgs. commercially frozen strawberries, thawed	2 x 283 g
12½ oz.	frozen lemonade concentrate, just thawed	355 mL
8 cups	club soda, chilled	2 L

Combine raspberries and strawberries. Simmer 5 minutes. Strain and chill. Combine lemonade concentrate and club soda; add to fruit liquid. Serve over crushed ice.
SERVES: 12.

Use fresh or whole frozen strawberries for punch bowl decorations.

Fruit Soup

3 tbsp.	sugar	50 mL
3 tbsp.	cornstarch	50 mL
1/8 tsp.	salt	0.5 mL
1 1/4 cups	sparkling red wine	300 mL
1 cup	water	250 mL
1 1/2 cups	cranberry juice	375 mL
3 cups	fresh strawberries or raspberries	750 mL

Combine sugar, cornstarch, salt, wine and water in a saucepan. Cook and stir. Simmer about 1 minute, then remove from heat; add cranberry juice. Cover and refrigerate. Strawberries or raspberries should be added when soup is served. Use soup the day it is prepared.
SERVES: 6.

Strawberry Soup

4 cups	fresh strawberries OR	1 L
4 cups	frozen whole strawberries, partly thawed	1 L
1 cup	orange juice	250 mL
2 tsp.	instant tapioca	10 mL
1/8 tsp.	allspice	0.5 mL
1/8 tsp.	cinnamon	0.5 mL
1/2 cup	sugar	125 mL
1 tsp.	grated lemon peel	5 mL
1 tbsp.	lemon juice	15 mL
1 cup	buttermilk	250 mL

Purée strawberries. Combine purée with orange juice in a saucepan. Remove about 1/4 cup (50 mL) of mixture and combine with the tapioca. Add tapioca mixture to purée in saucepan. Add allspice, cinnamon and sugar, and cook and stir until mixture thickens. Remove from heat; add lemon peel, lemon juice and buttermilk. Cover and refrigerate 8 hours or overnight.
SERVES: 4.

Raspberry Soup

3 cups	home-frozen unsweetened raspberries, thawed and drained, plus	750 mL
2 cups	juice from berries	500 mL
¼ cup	sugar,	50 mL
	OR	
4 x 10 oz.	pkgs. commercially frozen berries, thawed	4 x 283 g
2 cups	sweet wine	500 mL
2 x 2"	cinnamon sticks	2 x 5 cm
2 tsp.	cornstarch	10 mL
½ cup	water	125 mL

Combine first 3 ingredients or commercially frozen raspberries with wine and cinnamon sticks and simmer about 10 minutes. Combine cornstarch and water and slowly add to berry liquid. Simmer until mixture thickens. Remove cinnamon and refrigerate in covered container.
SERVES: 6.

Strawberry Soup — Blender Quick

½ cup	white wine	125 mL
½ cup	sugar	125 mL
2 tbsp.	lemon juice	25 mL
1 tsp.	grated lemon peel	5 mL
2 cups	strawberries, fresh	500 mL
	OR	
2 cups	whole frozen strawberries, partly thawed	500 mL

Combine all the ingredients in a blender and blend until smooth. Cover and refrigerate. When soup is made with partly thawed berries it is ready to serve without additional chilling.
SERVES: 3.

Fondues
Dips
Sauces

Fondue for Strawberries

A fondue consists of melting and blending of ingredients. For dipping have bite-size pieces of fresh pineapple, peaches, cake and always the beautiful strawberries. Wash and drain strawberries but leave caps and stems on.

Chocolate and Honey Fondue

1 cup	chocolate chips	250 mL
½ cup	cream or evaporated milk	125 mL
¼ cup	honey	50 mL

Carefully heat all ingredients until blended.

Mocha Fondue

1 cup	chocolate chips	250 mL
1 tbsp.	instant coffee	15 mL
¾ cup	cream or evaporated milk	175 mL
1 tbsp.	Tia Maria or Kahlúa, optional	15 mL

Carefully heat all ingredients until blended.

Strawberry Fondue

1 cup	cream or evaporated milk	250 mL
1 tbsp.	cornstarch	15 mL
¾ cup	strawberries, puréed	175 mL
½ cup	confectioner's icing sugar	125 mL

Combine cream and cornstarch. Add puréed strawberries and confectioner's icing sugar. Heat and blend until mixture thickens.

Serve with bite-size pieces of fruit, French bread, cake or biscuits. YIELDS: 2 cups (500 mL).

Candied Strawberries

24	strawberries, washed and drained, caps and stems on	24
3 cups	sugar	750 mL
½ cup	light corn syrup	125 mL
½ cup	water	125 mL

Pull back caps of berries and insert toothpick through hull, going almost to tip of berry. In a small, heavy saucepan combine sugar, corn syrup and water. Heat and stir until sugar dissolves and then cook rapidly, without stirring, to 285°F (145°C) on candy thermometer. (A teaspoon of syrup dropped into a cup of cold water will separate into hard strands). Remove from heat. Dip strawberries into syrup to coat entire berry. Lift berry from syrup and allow excess syrup to drain back into pan. Hold berry a few seconds until syrup hardens then cool on foil-covered wire rack. Berries should be kept at room temperature and served within 2 hours.
YIELDS: 24.

Fondant-Dipped Strawberries

2½ cups	confectioner's icing sugar	625 mL
3 tbsp.	lemon juice	50 mL
2 tbsp.	light corn syrup	25 mL
30	strawberries, washed and drained, caps and stems on	30

In top of double boiler combine confectioner's icing sugar, lemon juice and corn syrup. Cook and stir until mixture is smooth and a consistency that will coat a strawberry. Remove from heat but keep warm over hot water. Hold strawberry by stem and dip into mixture turning to cover entire strawberry. Dry the strawberries on wire racks placed on cookie sheets. Strawberries should dry for 1 hour but should not be stored overnight.
YIELDS: 30.

Cinnamon Cream Cheese Dip or Sauce

1 cup	cream cheese, softened	250 mL
2 tbsp.	brown sugar	25 mL
1 tsp.	cinnamon	5 mL

Combine all ingredients.
YIELDS: 1 cup (250 mL).

Custard Sauce To Serve With Strawberries or Raspberries

4	egg yolks, beaten	4
⅓ cup	sugar	75 mL
⅛ tsp.	salt	0.5 mL
2 cups	milk	500 mL
1 tsp.	vanilla	5 mL

In double boiler combine egg yolks, sugar, and salt. Gradually add milk and cook and stir until custard coats spoon. Remove from heat. Add vanilla.
YIELDS: 2¼ cups (550 mL).

Yogurt Sour Cream Dip

1 cup	yogurt	250 mL
1 cup	sour cream	250 mL
2 tbsp.	honey	25 mL
¾ tsp.	ground ginger	4 mL
½ tsp.	lemon juice	2 mL

Combine all ingredients. Cover and refrigerate 1 hour before serving.
YIELDS: 2 cups (500 mL).

Berry Topping

2 cups	frozen unsweetened strawberries or raspberries, thawed and drained	500 mL
¼ cup	juice from berries, above	50 mL
3	egg yolks	3
2 tbsp.	sugar	25 mL
⅛ tsp.	salt	0.5 mL
¼ tsp.	almond extract	1 mL
2 cups	whipped cream or prepared topping	500 mL

In top of double boiler combine the juice from berries, egg yolks, sugar and salt. Cook and stir until mixture is very thick. Add almond extract. Cover surface with waxed paper and refrigerate until chilled. Fold in whipped cream and berries.
YIELDS: 2¼ cups (550 mL).

Berry and Cherry Sauce

2 cups	frozen unsweetened strawberries or raspberries, thawed	500 mL
1 tsp.	lemon juice	5 mL
19 oz.	cherry pie filling	540 mL

Combine all ingredients and mix. With strawberries it's mellow; with raspberries it's more pungent.

Kahlúa Sour Cream Dip or Sauce

1 cup	sour cream	250 mL
2 tbsp.	brown sugar	25 mL
2 tbsp.	Kahlúa	25 mL

Combine all ingredients.
YIELDS: 1 cup.

Brandied Strawberry Sauce

3 cups	whole frozen strawberries, thawed and drained	750 mL
½ cup	juice from strawberries	125 mL
1 tbsp.	cornstarch	15 mL
½ cup	currant jelly	125 mL
¼ cup	brandy	50 mL

Combine juice from strawberries with cornstarch. Melt jelly in a saucepan and gradually add cornstarch mixture. Cook and stir until thickened. Carefully fold in strawberries and brandy. Cover and refrigerate.

YIELDS: 2½ cups (625 mL).

Brandied Raspberry Sauce

1 cup	pkg. home-frozen raspberries, thawed and drained, plus	250 mL
⅔ cup	juice from raspberries and water to yield	150 mL
	OR	
10 oz.	pkg. commercially frozen unsweetened raspberries, thawed and drained, plus	283 g
⅔ cup	juice from raspberries	150 mL
1 tbsp.	sugar	15 mL
1½ tsp.	cornstarch	7 mL
¼ cup	brandy or raspberry liqueur	50 mL

In saucepan combine juice from raspberries, sugar and cornstarch. Cook and stir until mixture thickens. Press raspberries through sieve to remove seeds. Add raspberries and brandy to the sauce.

YIELDS: 1 cup (250 mL).

Raspberry Sauce

½ cup	butter or margarine	125 mL
¾ cup	sugar	175 mL
1 cup	mashed raspberries	250 mL
1 tbsp.	cornstarch	15 mL
1 tbsp.	water, cold	15 mL
1	egg white, stiffly beaten	1

Melt butter in a saucepan. Add sugar and raspberries. Combine cornstarch and water and add to raspberry mixture. Cook and stir until mixture thickens. Remove from heat and cool. Fold in the stiffly beaten egg white.
YIELDS: 6.

Fruit Sauce

2 tbsp.	brown sugar	25 mL
1 tbsp.	cornstarch	15 mL
½ cup	orange juice	125 mL
¼ cup	water	50 mL
2 cups	fresh strawberries or raspberries	500 mL
2	bananas, sliced	2

Combine brown sugar, cornstarch, orange juice and water. Cook and stir until mixture thickens. Cover and refrigerate. At serving time fold in fruit.
SERVES: 4.

Fresh Strawberry Sauce

2 cups	sliced strawberries	500 mL
¼ cup	sugar	50 mL
1 tbsp.	lemon juice	15 mL
¼ tsp.	almond extract	1 mL

Combine strawberries, sugar and lemon juice in a saucepan. Simmer about 10 minutes. Add almond extract. Cool.
YIELDS: 1⅓ cups (325 mL).

Spiced Strawberry Sauce

2 cups	frozen strawberries, thawed and drained	500 mL
1 cup	juice from strawberries and water to yield	250 mL
2 tbsp.	cornstarch	25 mL
¼ cup	sugar	50 mL
½ tsp.	cloves	2 mL
½ tsp.	cinnamon	2 mL
½ tsp.	allspice	2 mL

Combine juice from strawberries, cornstarch and sugar. Cook and stir until mixture thickens. Add spices and fold in strawberries. Cover and refrigerate.

YIELDS: 2½ cups (625 mL).

Strawberry Rhubarb Sauce for Shortcake

3 cups	sliced rhubarb	750 mL
¾ cup	sugar	175 mL
⅛ tsp.	salt	0.5 mL
½ cup	water	125 mL
1½ tbsp.	cornstarch	22 mL
3 tbsp.	water	50 mL
3 cups	sliced strawberries	750 mL

Combine rhubarb, sugar, salt and water in saucepan. Bring to boil, reduce heat and simmer covered 5 minutes. Blend cornstarch with 3 tbsp. (50 mL) water. Stir into rhubarb, bring to boil. Reduce heat and cook and stir 2 minutes. Cool. Add the strawberries and chill.

SERVES: 8-12.

Salads

Honeydew and Berry Salad

1	honeydew melon	1
	salad greens	
¼ tsp.	ground ginger	1 mL
1 cup	strawberries	250 mL
½ cup	raspberries	125 mL
4	green grape clusters	4

Place honeydew wedges on salad greens of your choice. Sprinkle with ground ginger. Top with strawberries, raspberries and green grape clusters. The green grape clusters may be frosted by dipping in beaten egg white and then in sugar. Serve with your favorite dressing.
SERVES: 4.

Fresh Fruit and Yogurt Salad

3 cups	strawberries	750 mL
1	cantaloupe, cut in pieces	1
3	peaches, sliced	3
2	bananas, sliced	2
1 cup	white seedless grapes	250 mL
½ cup	shredded coconut	125 mL
2 cups	yogurt	500 mL
¼ cup	honey	50 mL
2 tsp.	vanilla	10 mL
¼ cup	sunflower seeds	50 mL

Combine fruits and coconut. In a blender combine yogurt, honey and vanilla and blend. Carefully fold yogurt mixture into the fruit. Garnish with sunflower seeds.
SERVES: 6.

1 cup (150 g) of strawberries equals 58 calories.

Strawberry Spinach Salad*

1 bunch	fresh spinach, washed and dried	1 bunch
1 cup	quartered fresh strawberries	250 mL

In a large salad bowl place fresh spinach and tear into bite-size pieces. Add strawberries. Toss lightly with commercial creamy coleslaw dressing, mayonnaise or a choice of dressings. Add a dash of salt and freshly ground pepper.
SERVES: 4.

Fruit and Nut Salad

3 cups	strawberries or raspberries	750 mL
1 cup	blueberries	250 mL
2 cups	thin slices of orange	500 mL
1 cup	coarsely chopped nuts	250 mL
1½ cups	yogurt	375 mL
⅓ cup	orange juice	75 mL
2 tbsp.	honey	25 mL
	salad greens	

Combine fruit and nuts. Combine yogurt, orange juice and honey and fold into fruit. Serve on salad greens.
SERVES: 6-8.

Strawberry Zucchini Salad

A different way to serve some of that plentiful zucchini!

	leaf lettuce	
1 cup	thinly sliced zucchini	250 mL
1½ cups	halved strawberries	375 mL

Place several pieces of leaf lettuce on salad plate. Add thin slices of zucchini and halved strawberries. Serve with your favorite dressing.
SERVES: 4.

Spring Salad

6 oz.	lime gelatin	170	g
¾ tsp.	salt	4	mL
1¾ cup	boiling water	425	mL
2 tbsp.	vinegar	25	mL
2 tbsp.	lemon juice	25	mL
¼ cup	water	50	mL
3	cucumbers, medium	3	
8 oz.	cream cheese, softened	250	g
1 cup	mayonnaise	250	mL
1 cup	strawberries or raspberries	250	mL

Dissolve gelatin and salt in boiling water; add vinegar and lemon juice. Take out ¾ cup (175 mL) of mixture and combine with ¼ cup (50 mL) of water. This will make a clear layer to be poured into a 6-cup (1.5 L) mold. Chill until almost set. Meanwhile prepare cucumber-cream cheese layer: pare cucumbers, halve, scrape out seeds. Use a fine blade on food chopper to mince the cucumber. Drain. Measure 1½ cups (375 mL) of drained ground cucumber. Combine cucumber with cream cheese and mayonnaise. Add remaining gelatin mixture. Chill until mixture thickens then carefully pour over clear layer. Chill until firm. To serve: unmold and fill center with fresh strawberries or raspberries.

NOTE: If a dish is used rather than a mold the clear layer should go on top.

I like to use this salad on a buffet table for special dinners. SERVES: 8.

BERRY QUICK STRAWBERRY TOSSED SALAD:
Combine bite-size pieces of your favorite salad greens and watercress. Add a few slices of red onion rings and sliced strawberries. Serve with oil and vinegar dressing.

Raspberry Ring

6 oz.	raspberry gelatin	170 g
2 cups	boiling water	500 mL
2 cups	vanilla ice cream	500 mL
¾ cup	frozen lemonade concentrate	175 mL
2 cups	home-frozen raspberries, thawed and drained	500 mL
	OR	
15 oz.	commercially frozen raspberries, thawed and drained	425 g
½ cup	juice from raspberries	125 mL
¼ cup	chopped nuts	50 mL

Dissolve gelatin in boiling water. Add ice cream in small amounts and stir until melted. Add lemonade concentrate and juice from raspberries. Chill until mixture thickens. Add raspberries and nuts. Pour into a 6-cup (1.5 L) ring mold or dish and chill until set.

SERVES: 8.

Jellied Fruit Salad

2 tbsp.	gelatin	25 mL
4 cups	white grape juice	1 L
1	banana, bias cut	1
1½ cups	cored and chopped apple	375 mL
1½ cups	whole frozen strawberries, thawed and drained	375 mL
⅔ cup	diced celery	150 mL

Soften gelatin in ½ cup (125 mL) of the grape juice. Add ½ cup (125 mL) of hot grape juice and stir until dissolved. Add remaining 3 cups (750 mL) of juice and chill until mixture thickens. Fold in prepared fruit and celery. Pour into 1½-quart (1.5 L) mold or dish. Refrigerate 5 hours or overnight.

SERVES: 8-10.

Strawberry Cranberry Salad

6 oz.	mixed fruit gelatin	170 g
2 cups	boiling water	500 mL
2 cups	frozen whole strawberries, thawed and drained	500 mL
1½ cups	juice from berries and water to yield	375 mL
1 cup	chopped celery	250 mL
1 cup	chopped nuts	250 mL
14 oz.	canned cranberry sauce, drained	398 mL

Dissolve gelatin in the boiling water. Add the juice. Set aside ¾ cup (175 mL) of this liquid for top of salad. Chill remaining gelatin mixture until it thickens. Fold in the strawberries, celery, nuts and cranberry sauce. Pour into 2-quart (2 L) dish and refrigerate. When mixture is set pour the ¾ cup (175 mL) of gelatin over the surface. Pour the liquid into a large spoon and let it run off spoon. This will help avoid making a hole in the salad. Chill until firm.

This recipe is perfect with a turkey dinner.
SERVES: 10-12.

Strawberry Buttermilk Salad

1 tbsp.	gelatin	15 mL
1 cup	buttermilk	250 mL
1 cup	orange juice	250 mL
3 tbsp.	honey	50 mL
1 cup	fresh or frozen blueberries	250 mL
1 cup	fresh strawberries	250 mL
	OR	
1 cup	frozen strawberries, thawed and drained	250 mL

Strawberries have a very high vitamin C content.

Strawberry Buttermilk Salad (cont'd)

Soften gelatin in buttermilk. Heat orange juice to boiling; add honey. Slowly add to buttermilk mixture and blend in covered blender. Chill until mixture thickens. Fold in blueberries and strawberries. Pour into 3-cup (750 mL) mold or dish. Refrigerate 5 hours.
SERVES: 4-6.

Delicious

16	marshmallows, large	16
1 cup	milk	250 mL
3 oz.	lime gelatin	85 g
6 oz.	cream cheese	170 g
14 oz.	pineapple, crushed style, drained	398 mL
¾ cup	juice from pineapple	175 mL
½ cup	mayonnaise	125 mL
3 cups	whole frozen strawberries, thawed and drained	750 mL
¾ cup	juice from strawberries and water to yield	175 mL
3 oz.	strawberry gelatin	85 g
1 cup	cold water	250 mL

In double boiler melt the marshmallows in the milk. Add lime gelatin and stir until dissolved. Add cream cheese and pineapple juice and mix. Chill until mixture starts to thicken; fold in pineapple and mayonnaise. Pour into 2-quart (2 L) dish. Refrigerate.

For second layer bring strawberry juice to a boil; add gelatin and stir to dissolve. Add cold water. Chill until mixture thickens, fold in strawberries. Carefully pour over first layer. Refrigerate.
SERVES: 12.

Strawberry and Blue Cheese Salad

FIRST LAYER:

1 tbsp.	gelatin	15 mL
¼ cup	cold water	50 mL
2 cups	cottage cheese, drained	500 mL
½ cup	liquid from cottage cheese and milk to yield	125 mL
2 tbsp.	blue cheese	25 mL

Soften gelatin in the cold water; dissolve over hot water. Combine cottage cheese, milk and blue cheese and blend well. Add gelatin mixture and blend. Pour into 2-quart (2 L) dish or mold. Refrigerate until almost set.

SECOND LAYER:

2 cups	frozen unsweetened, sliced strawberries, thawed and drained	500 mL
1 cup	juice from strawberries and water to yield	250 mL
¾ cup	cold water	175 mL
3 oz.	strawberry gelatin	85 g

Heat to boiling the 1 cup (250 mL) of juice to dissolve gelatin. Add cold water and chill until mixture thickens. Fold in strawberries. Carefully pour over top of salad. Refrigerate until firm. SERVES: 6-8.

 BERRY QUICK FRUIT SALAD:
Combine diced fresh pineapple, strawberries or raspberries and chopped mint. Arrange on salad greens.

Strawberries and Pretzels

From Florence Hayward, a dear friend from Ohio.

2 cups	crushed pretzels	500 mL
¾ cup	butter or margarine, melted	175 mL
4 tbsp.	sugar	50 mL
8 oz.	cream cheese, softened	250 g
1 cup	sugar	250 mL
1 cup	Cool Whip	250 mL
6 oz.	strawberry gelatin	170 g
2 cups	boiling water	500 mL
4 cups	frozen strawberries	1 L
1 tbsp.	coarsely grated orange peel	15 mL

Preheat oven to 400°F (200°C).

Combine crushed pretzels, melted butter and sugar. Pat into a 9" x 13" (22 cm x 33 cm) pan and bake 8 minutes. Cool.

Cream together the softened cream cheese, sugar and Cool Whip as it comes from the freezer. Spread over base.

Dissolve strawberry gelatin in boiling water. Add the strawberries and orange peel. Stir until the strawberries are thawed. Pour over cream cheese layer and refrigerate until serving time.

This may also be used as a dessert.
SERVES: 12-15.

BERRY QUICK VICE-VERSA:

On ice cream serve strawberries with melted raspberry jelly or raspberries with melted strawberry jelly.

Strawberry, Pineapple and Rhubarb Salad

4 cups	frozen rhubarb	1 L
14 oz.	crushed pineapple, drained	398 mL
1 cup	pineapple juice	250 mL
6 oz.	strawberry gelatin	170 g
1 tbsp.	lemon juice	15 mL
1 tbsp.	grated crystallized ginger	15 mL
1 cup	home-frozen strawberries, thawed and drained OR	250 mL
15 oz.	commercially frozen strawberries thawed and drained	425 g
⅔ cup	juice from strawberries	150 mL

Cook rhubarb in pineapple juice until tender. Add gelatin and stir until dissolved. Add lemon juice, ginger and juice from sraw-berries. Chill until mixture starts to thicken. Fold in pineapple and strawberries. Pour into 1½-quart (1.5 L) dish.
SERVES: 6

Jellied Strawberry Rhubarb Salad

½ cup	sugar	125 mL
¾ cup	hot water	175 mL
1	orange	1
4 cups	rhubarb, fresh or frozen, in 1" pieces	1 L
2 cups	home-frozen sliced unsweetened strawberries, thawed and drained, plus	500 mL
½ cup	juice from strawberries, plus	125 mL
¼ cup	sugar OR	50 mL
15 oz.	pkg. commercially frozen sliced sweetened strawberries, thawed	425 g
2 tbsp.	gelatin	25 mL
½ cup	cold water	125 mL

Jellied Strawberry Rhubarb Salad (cont'd)

Combine sugar and water. Slice the unpeeled orange into very thin slices; add to sugar water. Bring to boil; simmer 10 minutes. Add rhubarb; bring to boil, cover saucepan with lid and remove from heat. Let stand 20 minutes. Remove rhubarb with slotted spoon and place in blender. Add strawberries, plus juice and sugar if using home-frozen, and blend until smooth. Soften gelatin in cold water; dissolve in hot syrup. Combine all ingredients and pour into 6-cup (1.5 L) mold or dish and chill 5 hours or until set.

NOTE: Taste orange peel as some has a bitter flavor.
SERVES: 6-8.

Strawberry Chicken Salad in Pita Bread

2 cups	diced, cooked chicken	500 mL
1 cup	shredded lettuce	250 mL
¾ cup	white grapes, halved	175 mL
1 cup	strawberries, halved	250 mL
1 cup	sprouts	250 mL
4	pita bread pockets	4

Combine salad ingredients. Add choice of dressing and stuff into pita bread pockets.
SERVES: 4. See photograph page 16.

Some fresh fruits make natural and very attractive serving dishes for other fruits. Try a watermellon basket or pineapple boat.

Christmas Jellied Salad

FIRST LAYER:

2 cups	frozen strawberries, thawed and drained	500 mL
1½ cups	juice from strawberries and water to yield	375 mL
3 oz.	strawberry gelatin	85 g

Dissolve strawberry gelatin in 1 cup (250 mL) of hot juice; add remaining juice and chill until thick but not set. Add strawberries. Pour into 1½-quart (1.5 L) clear dish. Refrigerate until almost set.

SECOND LAYER:

14 oz.	crushed pineapple, well drained	398 mL
1¾ cups	pineapple juice and water to yield	425 mL
3 oz.	lime gelatin	85 g
½ cup	shredded Cheddar cheese	125 mL

Dissolve lime gelatin in 1 cup (250 mL) hot juice. Add remaining juice and chill until thick but not set. Add pineapple and shredded cheese. Carefully pour over first layer. Refrigerate until firm.

THIRD LAYER:

1 cup	whipped cream or whipped topping	250 mL
½ cup	chopped nuts	125 mL

Spread the whipped cream on top and sprinkle with chopped nuts.

SERVES: 8.

 BERRY QUICK HOLIDAY DESSERT:
Top pistachio pudding with strawberries or raspberries.

Strawberry or Raspberry Tuna Tossed Salad

1	lettuce, medium head	1
6.5 oz.	tuna, canned, drained	184 g
2 cups	strawberries, halved or raspberries	500 mL
1/4 cup	slivered almonds	50 mL
1 tbsp.	chopped parsley	15 mL

DRESSING:

2 tbsp.	orange juice	25 mL
1 tbsp.	grated orange peel	15 mL
1/2 cup	mayonnaise	125 mL
1/8 tsp.	salt	0.5 mL
1/8 tsp.	pepper	0.5 mL

Break lettuce into bite-size pieces. Put into salad bowl. Sprinkle tuna, strawberries or raspberries, nuts and parsley over lettuce.

Blend together the salad dressing ingredients. Add to the salad and gently toss.
SERVES: 4.

Strawberry Taco Salad

4 oz.	tortilla chips	125 g
2 cups	shredded lettuce	500 mL
1 cup	sour cream	250 mL
2	avocados	2
1 tbsp.	lemon juice	15 mL
1/4 tsp.	salt	1 mL
2 cups	strawberries, halved	500 mL
1/2 cup	shredded Cheddar cheese	125 mL

Serve as 1 large or 4 individual salads. Place tortilla chips on bottom of plate, sprinkle with shredded lettuce. Spoon sour cream over lettuce and then spoon on avocado which has been mashed with lemon juice and salt. Add strawberries and sprinkle shredded cheese over top.
SERVES: 4. See photograph page 16.

Strawberry Shrimp Salad

2 lbs.	cooked large shrimp, shelled and deveined	1 kg
2	papayas or melons, sliced	2
½	pineapple, cut into spears	½
2	avocados, sliced	2
2	kiwifruit, sliced	2
2 cups	strawberries	500 mL
	mint, optional	
	toasted coconut, slivered almonds or macadamia nuts	

Arrange shrimp and fruit on salad greens. Garnish with mint, if using. Serve salad dressing in an attractive dish. Have small dishes of toasted coconut, slivered almonds or macadamia nuts to pass with salad dressing.

SALAD DRESSING:

1 tbsp.	crystallized ginger	15 mL
½ cup	whipping cream	125 mL
2 tbsp.	lime juice	30 mL
1 tbsp.	grated lime rind	15 mL
2 tbsp.	honey	30 mL
¼ cup	mayonnaise	50 mL

Grate the ginger in blender. Add whipping cream, lime juice, rind, and honey and blend until fluffy. Fold mixture into mayonnaise.

SERVES: 6.

Strawberry growers would like to sell their strawberries at Japanese prices — $1.00 per berry.

Crêpes
Breads
Cookies
Bars

Banana Pancakes with Strawberry Sauce

1¾ cup	flour	425 mL
2½ tsp.	baking powder	12 mL
¼ tsp.	salt	1 mL
4 tbsp.	brown sugar	50 mL
1	egg, beaten	1
1¾ cup	milk	425 mL
1 tsp.	vanilla	5 mL
3 tbsp.	margarine, melted	50 mL
2	bananas	2

Sift together flour, baking powder and salt. Add brown sugar. Mix together beaten egg, milk, vanilla and margarine. Add liquid to dry ingredients. Cut bananas into thin slices; add to batter. Make pancakes as usual and serve with Strawberry Sauce below.

STRAWBERRY SAUCE:

2 cups	frozen unsweetened strawberries, thawed and drained	500 mL
1 cup	juice from strawberries and water to yield	250 mL
3 tbsp.	cornstarch	50 mL
¾ cup	sugar	175 mL
2 tbsp.	lemon juice	25 mL

Combine juice, cornstarch and sugar. Cook until thick. Add lemon juice and strawberries. Serve warm on pancakes.
YIELDS: 16 pancakes.

The strawberry is picked with cap or hull on. The ripe raspberry will pull off the standard of the plant. The blackberry does not separate from the standard.

Cheryl's Crêpes

6	eggs	6
1½ cups	flour	375 mL
¼ cup	sugar	50 mL
1 tsp.	salt	5 mL
2 tbsp.	margarine, melted	25 mL
1½ cups	milk	375 mL

Beat eggs until fluffy, about 3 minutes. Stir in flour, sugar and salt. Stir in margarine and milk. Grease skillet, heat and pour in batter to coat bottom. Tilt skillet so batter covers bottom evenly. Cook on both sides.

Cheryl serves her crêpes sprinkled with confectioner's icing sugar and the centers filled with whipped cream and strawberries, then rolled and garnished with a beautiful, fresh, whole strawberry.
YIELDS: 10-12 in 10" (25 cm) pan.

Strawberry or Raspberry Whipped Cream for Crêpes or Pancakes

2 cups	strawberries, sliced or raspberries	500 mL
¼ cup +	confectioner's icing sugar	50 mL +
1 cup	whipping cream	250 mL
2 tbsp.	orange liqueur OR	25 mL
1 tbsp.	vanilla	15 mL

Sweeten berries to taste with confectioner's icing sugar. Set aside. Beat the ¼ cup (50 mL) of confectioner's icing sugar, whipping cream and orange liqueur or vanilla until stiff. Serve the whipped cream filling and berries on crêpes or pancakes.
SERVES: 5.

¾ cup (100 g) or red raspberries equals 58 calories.

Strawberry Cottage Cheese Filling for Crêpes

3 cups	strawberries, fresh	750 mL
	OR	
3 cups	whole frozen strawberries, thawed and drained	750 mL
1 cup	cottage cheese, low fat	250 mL
1 tbsp.	sugar	15 mL
½ tsp.	vanilla	2 mL

Combine in mixer or blender 1 cup (250 mL) strawberries, cottage cheese, sugar and vanilla. Mix until smooth. If fresh strawberries are used the remaining 2 cups (500 mL) should be sliced. Place strawberries in crêpes and serve with the sauce.
SERVES: 8.

Sandwich Loaf

1 loaf	unsliced brown bread	1 loaf
10 oz.	whipped cream cheese	283 g
1 cup	crushed pineapple, drained	250 mL
¼ cup	sunflower seeds	50 mL
6 oz.	Gouda cheese, thinly sliced	170 g
3	kiwifruit, sliced	3
1 cup	strawberries, sliced	250 mL

Remove crusts from bread. Slice horizontally into 3 layers. Spread each layer with whipped cream cheese. On bottom layer spread crushed pineapple and sprinkle with sunflower seeds, on second layer the sliced cheese, on top layer sliced kiwifruit and strawberries. Stack slices together. Refrigerate. At serving time cut into 2" (5 cm) pieces.

NOTE: Freeze the bread crusts to be used in dressing or bread pudding.
SERVES: 5.

Berry Blintz Sandwiches

1½ cups	creamed cottage cheese	375 mL
1	egg	1
2 tbsp.	sugar	25 mL
12 slices	bread, white or whole-wheat	12 slices
3	eggs	3
⅓ cup	milk	75 mL
2 cups	home-frozen strawberries or raspberries, thawed OR	500 mL
2 x 10 oz.	pkgs. commercially frozen strawberries or raspberries, thawed sugar, optional	2 x 283 g

Combine cottage cheese, 1 egg and sugar until well mixed. Spread 6 slices of bread with the mixture and cover with remaining slices. In shallow dish combine 3 eggs and milk and mix. Preheat large skillet with butter. Dip sandwiches into egg mixture on 1 side and then the other. Cook in skillet, browning both sides. Keep warm in oven until all are browned. Serve with strawberries or raspberries. Adjust sugar to taste.
SERVES: 6.

Strawberry Sandwich

½ cup	cottage cheese	125 mL
¼ cup	sour cream	50 mL
2 oz.	cream cheese	55 g
8 slices	bread of choice	8 slices
1½ cups	sliced strawberries	375 mL

Combine and mix well the cottage cheese, sour cream and cream cheese. Spread about 2 tbsp. (25 mL) mixture on bread. Cut bread as desired. Top with overlapping slices of strawberries.
SERVES: 8.

Coffee Cake with Jam

2 cups	flour, sifted	500 mL
4 tsp.	baking powder	20 mL
1 tbsp.	sugar	15 mL
½ tsp.	salt	2 mL
⅓ cup	shortening	75 mL
¼ cup	milk	50 mL
1	egg, beaten	1
¾ cup	strawberry or raspberry jam	175 mL
¼ cup	brown sugar	50 mL
¼ cup	chopped nuts	50 mL
1 tbsp.	butter or margarine	15 mL
¼ tsp.	cinnamon	1 mL

Preheat oven to 400°F (200°C).

Sift together flour, baking powder, sugar and salt. Cut in shortening to a coarse crumb mixture. Set aside ¾ cup (175 mL) crumbs for topping. Combine milk and egg; add to crumb mixture stirring only until moistened. Pat into greased 8″ x 8″ (20 cm x 20 cm) pan. Spread with jam.

Combine reserved crumbs and remaining ingredients to make topping; sprinkle over jam. Bake 20 to 25 minutes.
SERVES: 9.

Harvest Muffins

2½ cups	flour	625 mL
½ cup	sugar	125 mL
2 tbsp.	butter or margarine	25 mL
2 tbsp.	lard	25 mL
2½ tsp.	cream of tartar	12 mL
1¼ tsp.	baking soda	6 mL
½ tsp.	salt	2 mL
1 cup	milk	250 mL
	butter for spreading	
	sugar	

Harvest Muffins (cont'd)

Preheat oven to 375°F (190°C).

Combine first 8 ingredients to make a soft dough. Roll out dough to ½" (1 cm) thickness. Spread with butter and sprinkle with sugar; roll as for jelly roll and cut into equal pieces. Place in 9" x 13" (22 cm x 33 cm) pan. Place 1 tsp. (5 mL) jam filling (below) on each piece. Bake 25-30 minutes.

FILLING:

¼ cup	butter or margarine, melted	50 mL
¼ cup	sugar	50 mL
½-¾ cup	strawberry or raspberry jam	125-175 mL

Combine all ingredients.
SERVES: 8-10.

Strawberry Bread

3 cups	flour	750 mL
1 tsp.	baking soda	5 mL
1 tsp.	salt	5 mL
1 tbsp.	cinnamon	15 mL
1½ cups	sugar	375 mL
4	eggs, beaten	4
1¼ cups	salad oil	300 mL
2 cups	thawed and drained frozen strawberries, (takes about 1 quart [1 L] to yield 2 cups [500 mL] thawed)	500 mL
1½ cups	chopped nuts	375 mL

Preheat oven to 350°F (180°C).

Combine the dry ingredients. Combine eggs and oil. Blend the dry ingredients and the egg mixture until just moistened. Fold in strawberries and nuts. Bake in 2 greased 9" x 5" (22 cm x 12 cm) loaf pans about 1 hour.

YIELDS: 2, 9" x 5" (22 cm x 12 cm) loaves.

Strawberry Rhubarb Coffee Cake

FILLING: Prepare first so it can cool.

3 cups	frozen sliced strawberries, thawed	750 mL
3 cups	frozen diced rhubarb	750 mL
2 tbsp.	lemon juice	25 mL
1 cup	sugar	250 mL
⅓ cup	cornstarch	75 mL

Combine strawberries and rhubarb in saucepan. Cover and cook about 5 minutes. Add lemon juice, sugar and cornstarch and cook until thick. Cool.

TOPPING:

¾ cup	sugar	175 mL
½ cup	flour	125 mL
¼ cup	butter or margarine	50 mL

Combine sugar and flour. Cut in butter to make fine crumbs.

BATTER:

3 cups	flour	750 mL
1 cup	sugar	250 mL
1 tsp.	baking soda	5 mL
1 tsp.	baking powder	5 mL
1 tsp.	salt	5 mL
1 cup	butter or margarine	250 mL
1 cup	buttermilk	250 mL
2	eggs, slightly beaten	2
1 tsp.	vanilla	5 mL

Preheat oven to 350°F (180°C).

Sift together flour, sugar, soda, baking powder and salt. Cut in butter to make fine crumbs. Beat together the buttermilk, eggs, and vanilla. Add to dry ingredients and stir until just moistened. Spread ½ batter in greased 9" x 13" (22 cm x 33 cm) pan. Carefully spread strawberry-rhubarb filling over batter. Spoon remaining batter in small mounds over filling. Sprinkle topping over all. Bake 40 to 45 minutes.
SERVES: 12-15.

Jam Cushions

8 oz.	cream cheese	250 g
1 cup	butter or margarine	250 mL
2 cups	flour, sifted	500 mL
1 cup	finely chopped nuts	250 mL
1 cup	strawberry or raspberry jam	250 mL

Preheat oven to 400°F (200°C).

Blend cream cheese and butter and stir in flour to make a dough. Chill 3 hours. Prepare filling by combining the nuts and jam. When dough has chilled divide into 4 pieces and work with one piece at a time. Roll out thin and cut into 2" (5 cm) circles. Top center of the circle with scant 1 tsp. (5 mL) of nut and jam mixture. Cover with another circle and seal edges by pressing with a fork. Bake 12 to 15 minutes.

YIELDS: 4 dozen. See photograph page 32.

Jam Turnovers

2 cups	flour	500 mL
1 tbsp.	baking powder	15 mL
2 tbsp.	sugar	25 mL
1 tsp.	salt	5 mL
1 cup	butter or margarine	250 mL
1	egg	1
½ cup	milk	125 mL
1 tsp.	vanilla	5 mL
1 cup	strawberry or raspberry jam	250 mL

Preheat oven to 375°F (190°C).

Mix flour, baking powder, sugar, salt and butter as for pie crust. Beat together the egg, milk and vanilla. Add to dry mixture. Roll out and cut in circles with 3" (7 cm) cutter. Place ½ tsp. (2 mL) jam on circle, fold over and pinch together. Bake about 10 minutes or until light brown.

YIELDS: 36. See photograph page 32.

Dream Bars

CRUST:

1 cup	flour	250 mL
¾ tsp.	soda	4 mL
¼ tsp.	salt	1 mL
1 cup	rolled oats	250 mL
½ cup	brown sugar	125 mL
½ cup	butter or margarine	125 mL

FILLING:

1 cup	strawberry or raspberry jam	250 mL

TOPPING:

2	eggs, beaten	2
1 cup	brown sugar	250 mL
½ cup	coconut	125 mL
½ cup	chopped nuts	125 mL

Preheat oven to 350°F (180°C).

Combine the first 6 ingredients to make a crumb mixture. Pat into a greased 9" x 13" (22 cm x 33 cm) pan. Spread jam on top. Combine the eggs, brown sugar and coconut and carefully pour over the jam. Sprinkle nuts on top. Bake about 30 minutes. YIELDS: 54 squares. See photograph page 32.

Cheese Squares

½ cup	butter or margarine	125 mL
½ cup	grated Velveeta cheese	125 mL
¼ cup	brown sugar	50 mL
1¾ cups	flour	425 mL
1½ tsp.	baking powder	7 mL
½ tsp.	salt	2 mL
½ cup	strawberry or raspberry jam	125 mL

Cheese Squares (cont'd)

Preheat oven to 300°F (150°C).

Combine all the ingredients except the jam to form a crumb mixture. Pat ¾ of mixture into 8" x 8" (20 cm x 20 cm) pan. Spread with the jam. Sprinkle the rest of the crumb mixture over the top. Bake about 25 minutes.
YIELDS: 25 pieces. See photograph page 32.

Granny's Cookies

1 cup	lard	250 mL
1 cup	margarine	250 mL
8 cups	flour	2 L
¾ cup	sugar	175 mL
½ tsp.	soda	2 mL
1 tsp.	baking powder	5 mL
⅛ tsp.	salt	0.5 mL
3	eggs	3
1 cup	evaporated milk	250 mL
1 tbsp.	lemon juice	15 mL
1 cup	strawberry or raspberry jam	250 mL

Preheat oven to 350°F (180°C).

Combine lard, margarine, flour, sugar, soda, baking powder and salt as for pie dough. Stir in eggs, milk and lemon juice. Roll out and cut with favorite cookie cutter. Bake about 10 minutes. Cool. Spread 1 cookie with jam and top with another cookie.

These cookies seem best the second day as they absorb the jam. They can be cut with a large cutter for the "man-size" appetite.
YIELDS: 4 dozen sandwiches. See photograph page 45.

Jam Bars

CRUST:

1 cup	flour, sifted	250 mL
1 tsp.	baking powder	5 mL
½ cup	butter or margarine	125 mL
1	egg	1

FILLING:

1 cup	strawberry or raspberry jam	250 mL

TOPPING:

¾ cup	sugar	175 mL
1 tbsp.	butter	15 mL
1	egg	1
2 cups	coconut	500 mL

Preheat oven to 325°F (160°C).

Combine all crust ingredients and pat into bottom of greased 9" x 13" (22 cm x 33 cm) pan. Spread with the jam.

Mix topping and carefully spoon over the jam. Bake about 30 minutes, until brown.

YIELDS: 54 bars.

Fruit Leather

2 cups	strawberry or raspberry purée	500 mL
1 cup	applesauce	250 mL
1 tbsp.	lemon juice	15 mL
¼ cup	sugar	50 mL

Preheat oven to 200°F (95°C).

Both the strawberry and the raspberry plants belong to the rose family.

Fruit Leather (cont'd)

Thaw, drain and purée berries to yield 2 cups (500 mL). Raspberries could be sieved to remove seeds if so desired. Add applesauce, lemon juice and sugar. Prepare a 10" x 15" (25 x 38 cm) jelly roll pan by lining with plastic wrap. Tape edges to sides and ends of pan. Pour fruit leather mixture into pan and spread evenly. Bake about 5 hours or until leather will pull away from plastic wrap. Empty leather onto counter, peel off plastic wrap. Remove any mixture that is not "set". Re-roll leather in fresh plastic wrap. Cut into 6 slices and wrap edges in plastic wrap. Great for lunches or a snack.

NOTE: This recipe must be baked at a low temperature.
SERVES: 6.

Walnut Meringue Bars

1 cup	butter	250 mL
½ cup	sugar	125 mL
1	egg yolk	1
½ tsp.	salt	2 mL
2½ cups	flour, sifted	625 mL
1 cup	strawberry or raspberry jam	250 mL
4	egg whites	4
1 cup	sugar	250 mL
1 tsp.	almond extract	5 mL
¾ cup	finely ground nuts	175 mL

Preheat oven to 350°F (180°C).

Cream butter and ½ cup (125 mL) sugar. Add egg yolk, salt and flour and combine. Pat into a 10" x 15" (25 x 38 cm) jelly roll pan. Spread jam over base. Beat egg whites until foamy and gradually add, while beating, the 1 cup (250 mL) sugar. Beat until stiff peaks form. Add almond extract and ground nuts. Spread meringue over jelly layer, sealing to edge of dough. Bake 35 to 40 minutes until browned. Cut into squares while warm.

YIELDS: 36 squares. See photograph page 47.

Strawberry Rhubarb Bars

CRUST:

1¾ cups	flour	425 mL
2 tbsp.	confectioner's icing sugar	25 mL
½ cup	butter or margarine	125 mL

FILLING:

1½ cups	sugar	375 mL
¼ cup	flour	50 mL
¼ tsp.	salt	1 mL
6	egg yolks	6
1 cup	evaporated milk	250 mL
4 cups	fresh rhubarb or frozen unsweetened, thawed and drained	1 L
2 cups	frozen unsweetened strawberries, thawed and drained	500 mL
½ tsp.	lemon juice	2 mL

MERINGUE:

6	egg whites	6
½ cup	sugar	125 mL

Preheat oven to 350°F (180°C).

To make crust, mix flour and sugar, cut in butter until mixture resembles coarse crumbs. Press into 9" x 13" (22 x 33 cm) pan. Bake until golden brown, 10-12 minutes.

To prepare filling, mix sugar, flour and salt in large bowl. Add slightly beaten egg yolks, and milk. Stir in rhubarb, strawberries and lemon juice. Spread evenly over crust. Bake until firm, about 1 hour.

Beat egg whites until foamy. Gradually add sugar, beating continuously until stiff peaks will hold. Spread over filling, return to oven. Bake until golden brown, about 10 minutes.
SERVES: 12-15

Cakes
Cream
Puffs
Custards
Frozen
Desserts
Shortcakes
Pizza

Strawberry Fluff Roll

A pretty dessert that isn't too sweet.

¾ cup	cake flour	175 mL
¼ tsp.	salt	1 mL
1 tsp.	baking powder	5 mL
4	egg yolks	4
¼ cup	sugar	50 mL
½ tsp.	vanilla	2 mL
4	egg whites	4
½ cup	sugar	125 mL
FILLING:		
1 tbsp.	gelatin	15 mL
¼ cup	cold water	50 mL
½ cup	hot water	125 mL
1 cup	fresh strawberries	250 mL
	OR	
1 cup	frozen strawberries, thawed and drained	250 mL
¼ cup	sugar	50 mL
1 tbsp.	lemon juice	15 mL
2 cups	whipping cream, whipped	500 mL

Preheat oven to 375°F (190°C).

Sift first 3 ingredients together, set aside. Beat egg yolks until thick. Gradually add ¼ cup (50 mL) sugar and vanilla, continue beating until thick and lemon-colored. Beat egg whites to soft peaks. Gradually add ½ cup (125 mL) sugar, beat until stiff peaks form. Fold yolk mixture into white mixture, then fold in the sifted dry ingredients. Grease a 10" x 15" (25 x 38 cm) jelly roll pan; line with waxed paper, regrease. Pour in the batter; bake 12-15 minutes. Turn onto dry cloth. Remove paper and roll up. Cool.

To prepare filling, soften gelatin in cold water, dissolve in the hot water. Add strawberries, sugar and lemon juice. Chill until partly set then beat until light and fluffy. Fold in whipped cream. Chill 10 minutes or until almost set.

When cake is cool, unroll and spread with ½ of filling. Use other ½ on outside of roll. Chill. Decorate with fresh strawberries. SERVES: 8.

Angel Cake Surprise

10"	whole angel food cake	25 cm

FILLING:

1 tbsp.	gelatin	15 mL
2 cups	home-frozen unsweetened strawberries, thawed and drained, plus	500 mL
¼ cup	juice from strawberries, plus	50 mL
½ cup	sugar	125 mL
	OR	
15 oz.	pkg. purchased sweetened strawberries, thawed and drained, plus	425 g
¼ cup	juice from strawberries	50 mL
1 tbsp.	gelatin	15 mL
1 tbsp.	lemon juice	15 mL
1	egg white, beaten stiff	1
1 cup	whipping cream, whipped	250 mL

ICING:

2 cups	whipping cream	500 mL
¼ cup	Grand Marnier	50 mL

Cut off the top and hollow out cake.

To prepare filling, soften gelatin in juice from strawberries. Dissolve over hot water. Purée strawberries, adding sugar if using unsweetened strawberries. Add lemon juice. Combine gelatin and strawberry mixture and chill until mixture thickens. Fold in beaten egg white and the whipped cream. Fill hollow of cake with strawberry mixture.

Whip the cream with the Grand Marnier. Cover sides of cake with the mixture. Use pastry bag to decorate top of cake with the mixture. Chill.

SERVES: 8.

Raspberry Layer Cake

4 cups	home-frozen unsweetened raspberries, thawed and drained, plus	1 L
¼ cup	sugar	50 mL
	OR	
2 x 10 oz.	pkgs. purchased frozen sweetened raspberries, thawed and drained	2 x 283 g
¼ cup	juice from raspberries	50 mL
1½ tsp.	gelatin	7 mL
2½ cups	whipping cream	625 mL
¾ cup	confectioner's icing sugar, sifted	175 mL
1	angel food or chiffon cake	1

Combine raspberry juice and gelatin to soften gelatin; then dissolve over hot water. Cool. Whip the cream until thick, add gelatin mixture and continue whipping until stiff. Continue beating and gradually add confectioner's icing sugar. Fold in drained berries. Slice the cake into 5 horizontal layers. Use ½ of filling for between layers and the remaining for covering outside of cake. Chill several hours.
SERVES: 12-16.

Strawberry Butter Cream Icing

⅓ cup	soft butter	75 mL
3 cups	confectioner's icing sugar, sifted	750 mL
3-4 tbsp.	crushed fresh or frozen thawed strawberries	50-65 mL

Blend together the butter and icing sugar. Stir in crushed strawberries.
YIELD: For 2, 9" (22 cm) layers or 9" x 13" (22 x 33 cm) pan.

Nut Torte

TORTE:

2½ cups	pecans	625 mL
2 tbsp.	flour	25 mL
6	eggs, separated	6
1 cup	sugar	250 mL
1 tsp.	vanilla	5 mL
1 tsp.	grated orange peel	5 mL

ORANGE ICING:

½ cup	butter, softened	125 mL
1 cup	confectioner's icing sugar	250 mL
4 tbsp.	orange-flavored liqueur	50 mL
4 tbsp.	grated orange peel	50 mL

TOPPING:

4 cups	sliced strawberries or raspberries	1 L

Preheat oven to 350°F (180°C).

Chop nuts finely in a blender. Add the flour and mix. Beat the egg yolks until light; gradually add sugar and continue beating about 5 minutes. Beat in vanilla. Fold in nut mixture and orange peel. Beat the egg whites to moist stiff peaks. Fold about ¼ of egg whites into egg yolk mixture. Fold in remaining whites until no large lumps of white remain. Pour into greased 10″ (25 cm) springform pan. Bake 45 minutes or until center tests done. Cool on rack. Remove outside of springform pan. Torte can be left on bottom of springform pan or transferred to tray.

Make orange icing by beating all ingredients together and cover torte. At serving time add strawberries.

If using frozen defrosted berries add to each piece when serving torte.
SERVES: 12.

Strawberry or Raspberry Torte

A favorite from Gruenke's Berry and Honey Farm, Emerson, Manitoba.

½ cup	butter	125 mL
½ cup	sugar	125 mL
2	eggs	2
⅓ cup	milk	75 mL
2 tsp.	baking powder	10 mL
1½ cups	flour, sifted	375 mL
⅛ tsp.	salt	0.5 mL
1 tsp.	vanilla	5 mL

FRUIT TOPPING:

2 cups	home-frozen strawberries or raspberries, thawed and drained, plus	500 mL
1 cup	juice from berries and water to yield	250 mL
	OR	
15 oz.	pkg. commercially frozen strawberries or raspberries, thawed and drained, plus	425 g
1 cup	juice from berries and water to yield	250 mL
2 tbsp.	cornstarch	25 mL
¼ cup	sugar	50 mL
2 cups	whipped cream or whipped topping	500 mL

Preheat oven to 375°F (190°C).

Cream butter and sugar. Add eggs and mix. Add milk and remaining ingredients, mix. Spoon into well greased 10" (25 cm) torte pan. Bake 20 minutes. Cool. Prepare topping.

Combine juice, cornstarch and sugar. Cook and stir until mixture thickens. Cool. Add berries. Cover top of torte with fruit mixture. Use pastry bag to decorate top with whipped cream.

NOTE: if sweetened berries are used adjust sugar.
SERVES: 8-10.

Himmel Torte

1½ cups	butter or margarine	375 mL
¼ cup	sugar	50 mL
4	egg yolks	4
4 cups	flour	1 L
1 tsp.	grated lemon peel	5 mL
1	egg white	1
¼ cup	sugar	50 mL
1 tsp.	cinnamon	5 mL
½ cup	almonds, chopped	125 mL

FILLING:

1 cup	raspberry jam	250 mL
2 cups	sour cream	500 mL
1 tbsp.	cornstarch	15 mL
¼ cup	sugar	50 mL
2	egg yolks, well-beaten	2
½ tsp.	vanilla	2 mL

Preheat oven to 450°F (250°C).

Cream butter and sugar; beat in egg yolks 1 at a time. Add flour and lemon peel and mix. Pat into 2 greased 10″ (25 cm) pans. Brush tops with mixture of egg white, sugar and cinnamon. Sprinkle with almonds. Bake 10-12 minutes. If not completely baked reduce heat to 350°F (180°C) and bake until well browned. Cool. Spread raspberry jam over bottom layer. Combine sour cream, cornstarch and sugar. Cook and stir over medium heat about 5 minutes. Gradually pour into the egg yolks. Reheat for 1 minute. Add vanilla. Spread ½ of filling over jam. Add second layer and spread with remaining filling.
SERVES: 12-15.

BERRY QUICK BERRY TORTONI:
Combine crumbled macaroon cookies, Amaretto liqueur or almond extract, whipped cream and strawberries or raspberries, freeze until firm.

Strawberry Torte

PASTRY:

2 cups	flour	500 mL
¼ cup	sugar	50 mL
1 cup	butter or margarine	250 mL
3	egg yolks	3

FILLING:

3 cups	frozen, unsweetened strawberries, thawed and drained	750 mL
1 cup	juice from strawberries and water to yield	250 mL
½ cup	sugar	125 mL
2 tbsp.	cornstarch	25
½ tsp.	almond extract	2 mL

TOPPING:

1 cup	whipping cream	250 mL
2 tbsp.	sugar	25 mL
1 tsp.	vanilla	5 mL
½ tsp.	almond extract	2 mL
½ cup	sliced almonds	125 mL

Preheat oven to 375°F (190°C).

Combine flour and sugar. Cut in butter to make coarse crumb mixture. Add egg yolks and combine. Press into bottom and 1½" (4 cm) up the sides of a 10" (25 cm) springform pan. Bake 20-25 minutes until light brown. Cool.

To prepare filling, combine juice from strawberries, sugar and cornstarch. Cook and stir until mixture thickens. Add almond extract. Place berries over bottom of tart shell. Carefully spoon filling over the strawberries. Chill. When well chilled carefully remove from springform pan and place on serving tray.

To prepare topping, whip the cream, fold in sugar and flavorings. Use pastry bag to decorate around edge of torte. Sprinkle the almonds on top of the whipped cream.

SERVES: 8-10. See photograph page 32.

Chocolate Torte

19 oz.	pkg. lemon cake mix	520 g
2	eggs	2

Preheat oven to 350°F (180°C).

Prepare cake as package directs using 2 eggs, and amount of water specified. Pour batter into prepared 10″ x 15″ (25 x 38 cm) pan that has been greased and lined with waxed paper. Bake 20 minutes or until surface springs back when lightly touched. Cool in pan 5 minutes then turn onto wire rack.

CHOCOLATE FILLING:

6 oz.	semisweet chocolate chips	170 g
6 oz.	cream cheese, softened	170 g
3 tbsp.	milk	50 mL
4 cups	confectioner's icing sugar	1 L
1/8 tsp.	salt	0.5 mL
1 tsp.	vanilla	5 mL
1/2 cup	raspberry or strawberry jam	125 mL
1/4 cup	slivered almonds	50 mL

Melt chocolate over hot water. In medium bowl blend cream cheese with milk. Gradually add sugar, beating until smooth. Beat in salt, vanilla and the melted chocolate.

Cut cake crosswise into 4 pieces 3″ x 10″ (7 x 25 cm). Place 1 piece on serving plate; spread with 1/4 cup (50 mL) jam. Top with second strip and spread with some of chocolate filling. Top with third strip and spread with remaining jam. Top with last strip and frost top and sides with remaining chocolate filling. Garnish with almonds. Refrigerate at least 1 hour before serving.
SERVES: 12-15.

Jam Torte

BASE:

1⅓ cups	flour, sifted	325 mL
1 cup	sugar	250 mL
1 tsp.	baking powder	5 mL
½ cup	butter or margarine, softened	125 mL
1	egg	1

FILLING:

½ cup	butter or margarine	125 mL
½ cup	sugar	125 mL
1 cup	ground almonds	250 mL
½ tsp.	almond extract	2 mL
2	eggs	2

TOPPING:

½ cup	strawberry or raspberry jam	125 mL

Mix flour, sugar and baking powder. Cut in butter, add egg. Press mixture into bottom and 1″ (3 cm) up the side of a 10″ (25 cm) springform pan. Cover and refrigerate while preparing filling. Preheat oven to 350°F (180°C).

In a mixing bowl combine all ingredients. Beat on low speed until well mixed and then on medium speed 3 minutes. Carefully pour batter into chilled crust. Bake 30 minutes or until toothpick inserted in center comes out clean. Cool on wire rack at least 1 hour. Remove side of springform pan. Spread on topping. SERVES: 10.

BERRY QUICK WHIPPED CREAM:
Add 2 tbsp. (25 mL) strawberry OR raspberry jam to 1 cup (250 mL) of whipped cream.

Cream Puffs

1 cup	water, boiling	250 mL
½ cup	butter	125 mL
1 cup	flour	250 mL
¼ tsp.	salt	1 mL
4	eggs	4

Preheat oven to 400°F (200°C).

In suacepan, add butter to boiling water. Combine flour and salt; add all at one time. Stir quickly until mixture is smooth and does not cling to sides of saucepan. Remove from heat. Add eggs 1 at a time. Beat well after each addition until mixture is smooth. Drop dough on ungreased baking tray about 3" (8 cm) apart. Bake 45 to 50 minutes until dry. Cream puffs can be split and returned to oven to dry centers. Cool. To serve, fill with Pink Lemonade Filling which follows.
YIELDS: 18, 3" (8 cm) puffs.

Pink Lemonade Filling For Cream Puffs

¾ cup	sugar	175 mL
⅛ tsp.	salt	0.5 mL
3 tbsp.	flour	50 mL
3 tbsp.	cornstarch	50 mL
6 oz.	frozen pink lemonade concentrate	170 g
1 cup	water	250 mL
2	egg yolks, slightly beaten	2
2 tbsp.	butter	25 mL
1½ cups	strawberries or raspberries	375 mL

In heavy saucepan mix together sugar, salt, flour and cornstarch. Combine pink lemonade concentrate and water and gradually add to sugar mixture. Cook and stir until mixture comes to a boil. Boil for 1 minute, stirring constantly. Remove from heat. Add a little of the hot mixture to beaten egg yolks. Gradually stir this mixture into hot mixture. Return to heat and cook and stir 1 minute; stir in the butter and set aside to cool. At serving time fill cream puffs with lemonade filling and berries.

Strawberry Rhubarb Crunch

BASE:

¾ cup	sugar	175 mL
1½ tbsp.	Minit tapioca	22 mL
1½ cups	whole frozen strawberries, thawed or drained	375 mL
½ cup	juice from strawberries and water to yield	125 mL
3 cups	diced rhubarb	750 mL

TOPPING:

¼ cup	butter or margarine, melted	50 mL
1 cup	quick-cooking rolled oats	250 mL
½ cup	flour	125 mL
¾ cup	brown sugar	175 mL
1 tsp.	cinnamon	5 mL
½ cup	chopped nuts	125 mL

Preheat oven to 375°F (190°C).

Combine base ingredients in 2-quart (2 L) baking dish. Let stand 5 minutes.

Combine topping ingredients and sprinkle over base. Bake about 25 minutes or until rhubarb is cooked.

SERVES: 6-8.

 BERRY QUICK BERRY TAPIOCA:

Place thawed frozen strawberries or raspberries in parfait glasses. Add tapioca pudding, more berries and pudding.

Strawberry Cobbler

4 cups	frozen strawberries, thawed and drained	1 L
1 cup	juice from strawberries and water to yield	250 mL
¾ cup	sugar	175 mL
2 tbsp.	cornstarch	25 mL
2 tbsp.	lemon juice	25 mL
½ tsp.	cinnamon	2 mL
2 cups	flour	500 mL
2 tbsp.	sugar	25 mL
1 tsp.	salt	5 mL
6 tbsp.	shortening	100 mL
½ cup	milk	125 mL

Preheat oven to 375°F (190°C).

Combine juice, sugar and cornstarch and cook until mixture thickens. Add lemon juice, cinnamon and strawberries. Pour into greased 1½-quart (1.5 L) casserole or baking pan. Combine remaining ingredients to make biscuit dough and drop by spoonfuls onto fruit. Bake 35-40 minutes.
SERVES: 6.

Elegant Custard

Thanks to Aunt Pheobe — one of the truly elegant ladies in Ohio.

4 cups	strawberries	1 L
¼ cup	anise-flavored liqueur or favorite liqueur	50 mL
¾ cup	flour	175 mL
4	eggs	4
1 cup	sugar	250 mL
4 cups	milk, boiling	1 L
1 cup	whipping cream	250 mL

Elegant Custard (cont'd)

Combine strawberries and liqueur and chill several hours. The strawberries may be slightly sweetened if desired.

In a saucepan combine flour, eggs and sugar. Slowly add the boiling milk. Use a wire whisk to combine. Cook and stir until mixture thickens. Cool. Whip the cream and use whisk to combine with custard. Layer strawberries and custard in your finest stemware.

Raspberries could be used in place of strawberries.
SERVES: 8.

Russian Cream with Strawberries Romanoff

RUSSIAN CREAM:

1 cup	heavy cream	250 mL
½ cup	sugar	125 mL
1 tbsp.	gelatin	15 mL
1 cup	sour cream	250 mL
½ tsp.	vanilla	2 mL

In saucepan mix together the heavy cream, sugar and gelatin. Heat on low until the gelatin is dissolved. Cool until mixture slightly thickens. Fold in sour cream and vanilla. Cover and chill at least 4 hours.

STRAWBERRIES ROMANOFF:

4 cups	fresh strawberries	1 L
½ cup	confectioner's icing sugar	125 mL
2 tbsp.	vodka	25 mL
2 tbsp.	Triple Sec	25 mL
2 tbsp.	rum	25 mL

Combine all ingredients and chill. At serving time spoon Russian Cream into your most beautiful dessert dishes. Top with Strawberries Romanoff.
SERVES: 4-6.

Cream-Filled Strawberries

To be used as a garnish, or served 4-5 in a fruit dish.

24	strawberries, large	24
1 cup	whipping cream	250 mL
2 tbsp.	almond or orange liqueur	25 mL
¼ cup	confectioner's icing sugar	50 mL

Wash and drain strawberries. Leave caps on. Slit each berry into quarters working toward cap but do not cut through cap. Whip the cream; add flavoring. Use pastry bag with star tip to fill the strawberries. Dust with icing sugar. Serve within 3 hours. YIELDS: 24.

Deluxe Bavarian

1	raspberry jam-filled jellyroll	1
3 tbsp.	gelatin	50 mL
¾ cup	cold water	175 mL
6 cups	fresh strawberries	1.5 L
	OR	
6 cups	whole frozen strawberries, thawed and drained	1.5 L
2 tbsp.	lemon juice	25 mL
3	eggs	3
⅛ tsp.	salt	0.5 mL
1 cup	sugar	250 mL
2 cups	whipping cream	500 mL

Soften gelatin in cold water, dissolve over hot water. Cool. Purée strawberries, add lemon juice and gelatin. Beat eggs and salt until frothy, add sugar gradually and beat until very light. Whip the cream until stiff. Fold strawberry and egg mixtures together. Fold in whipped cream.

Line sides of 10" (25 cm) springform pan with slices of jelly roll. Carefully pour strawberry mixture into pan. Refrigerate 8 hours or overnight.
SERVES: 12.

Strawberry Rhubarb Soufflé

RHUBARB SAUCE:

¾ cup	sugar	175 mL
2 tbsp.	water	25 mL
2 tbsp.	light corn syrup	25 mL
3 cups	rhubarb, in ½" (1.5 cm) pieces, fresh or frozen	750 mL

STRAWBERRY SOUFFLÉ:

1 cup	home-frozen strawberries, thawed and drained OR	250 mL
10 oz.	pkg. commercially frozen strawberries, thawed and drained	283 g
¼ cup	juice from strawberries	50 mL
1 tbsp.	gelatin	15 mL
1 tbsp.	lemon juice	15 mL
4	egg whites	4
¼ cup	sugar	50 mL
1 cup	whipping cream	250 mL

Prepare rhubarb sauce by combining sugar, water and corn syrup. Bring to a boil, cook and stir until sugar is dissolved. Add rhubarb and cover container. Cook over low heat until rhubarb is just tender. Cool. Prepare 6 cup (1.5 L) soufflé dish with collar and pour rhubarb sauce in bottom.

Soften gelatin in strawberry juice and let stand 5-10 minutes. Dissolve over hot water. Cool. Combine gelatin with strawberries and lemon juice and stir. Beat egg whites until foamy. Gradually beat in sugar until soft peaks form. In another bowl whip the cream. Fold meringue into strawberry mixture. Fold whipped cream (¾ cup [175 mL] may be saved to decorate top) into strawberry meringue mixture. Refrigerate until firm.

To serve, remove collar and garnish with remaining whipped cream. Dip to bottom of dish for rhubarb sauce to be spooned over each serving.
SERVES: 6.

Dessert Pizza with Fresh Fruit p. 86

Raspberry Dessert

FIRST LAYER:

9" x 13"	wafer crust of choice, minus:	22 x 33 cm
¼ cup	crumbs for top, reserved from crust mixture	50 mL

SECOND LAYER:

8 oz.	cream cheese	250 g
¼ cup	confectioner's icing sugar	50 mL
1 tsp.	vanilla	5 mL
⅛ tsp.	salt	0.5 mL

THIRD LAYER:

3 oz.	raspberry gelatin	85 g
1 cup	boiling water	250 mL
1 tbsp.	lemon juice	15 mL
2 cups	home-frozen raspberries, thawed and drained	500 mL
⅔ cup	juice from raspberries	150 mL
	OR	
15 oz.	pkg. commercially frozen raspberries, thawed and drained	425 g
⅔ cup	juice from raspberries	150 mL

TOPPING:

2 cups	whipping cream, whipped reserved crumbs (see above)	500 mL

Combine all ingredients of second layer and beat until smooth. Carefully spread on crumb base. If mixture is too thick add a small amount of cream. Prepare third layer.

Dissolve gelatin in boiling water. Add lemon juice, raspberries and juice. Combine and chill until mixture thickens. Spread over cream cheese mixture. Spread whipped cream on top of raspberry layer. Sprinkle with crumbs. Refrigerate.
SERVES: 12-15.

Berry Bavarian

9" x 13"	crust of choice	22 x 33 cm
4 cups	frozen strawberries or raspberries, thawed and drained	1 L
2 cups	juice from berries and water to yield	500 mL
6 oz.	mixed fruit gelatin	170 g
2 tbsp.	gelatin	25 mL
12 oz.	frozen orange juice concentrate, thawed	355 mL
⅔ cup	cold water	150 mL
4 cups	vanilla ice cream, softened	1 L

Heat 1 cup (250 mL) of the berry juice to dissolve the mixed fruit gelatin. Add plain gelatin to the remaining juice to soften then combine. Add orange juice concentrate and cold water. Add softened ice cream and blend. Pour into prepared crust. Refrigerate 5-6 hours.
SERVES: 12-15.

Strawberry Dessert

9" x 13"	crumb crust of choice	22 x 33 cm
2 cups	whole frozen strawberries, thawed and drained	500 mL
¾ cup	juice from berries and water to yield	175 mL
3 oz.	strawberry gelatin	85 g
1¼ cups	sweetened condensed milk	300 mL
½ cup	lemon juice	125 mL
3 cups	miniature white marshmallows	750 mL
2 cups	whipped cream or whipped topping	500 mL

Strawberry Dessert (cont'd)

Heat the juice from the strawberries to boiling. Add strawberry gelatin. Add sweetened condensed milk and mix. Add strawberries, lemon juice and marshmallows. Fold in the whipped cream. Refrigerate 3 hours or until set.
SERVES: 12-15

Strawberry Peppermint Dessert

9" x 13"	crumb crust of choice	22 x 33 cm
½ cup	crushed peppermint stick candy	125 mL
¼ cup	sugar	50 mL
1½ tbsp.	gelatin	22 mL
1¼ cup	milk	300 mL
3	egg yolks, slightly beaten	3
¼ tsp.	salt	1 mL
few drops	red food coloring	few drops
2 cups	unsweetended strawberries, thawed, drained and puréed	500 mL
3	egg whites	3
¼ cup	sugar	50 mL
1 cup	whipping cream, whipped	250 mL

Measure ⅓ cup (75 mL) of crushed candy and combine it with ¼ cup (50 mL) sugar, gelatin, milk, egg yolks and salt. Cook and stir over low heat until gelatin dissolves and candy melts. Add a few drops of red food coloring to enhance color. Fold in puréed strawberries. Chill until partly set. Beat egg whites until soft peaks form; gradually add the ¼ (50 mL) cup sugar and beat to stiff peaks. Fold into gelatin mixture. Pour over prepared crust. Top with whipped cream and sprinkle with remaining crushed pepperming candy. Chill several hours.
SERVES: 12-15

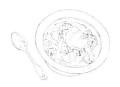

Strawberry Delight

9" x 13"	crumb crust of choice (reserve some crumb mixture for top of dessert)	22 x 33 cm
4 cups	whole frozen strawberries, thawed and drained	1 L
1 cup	juice from strawberries	250 mL
3 tbsp.	cornstarch	50 mL
½ cup	butter or margarine	125 mL
1 cup	confectioner's icing sugar	250 mL
2	eggs	2
½ tsp.	vanilla	2 mL
½ tsp.	almond extract	2 mL
2 cups	whipped cream or whipped topping	500 mL

Combine juice from strawberries and cornstarch. Cook and stir over low heat until mixture thickens. Set aside to cool. Cream butter and confectioner's icing sugar. Add eggs 1 at a time beating well after each addition. Add flavorings and pour over crust. Add strawberries to the thickened juice and pour over the egg-confectioner's icing sugar layer. Add the whipped cream and sprinkle with reserved crumb mixture. Refrigerate.
SERVES: 12-15.

Cheesecake

9" x 13"	crust of choice	22 x 33 cm
2 cups	whipping cream	500 mL
2 cups	sour cream	500 mL
1½ cups	sugar	375 mL
2 tbsp.	gelatin	25 mL
½ cup	water	125 mL
16 oz.	cream cheese, softened	500 g
1 tsp.	vanilla	5 mL
¼ tsp.	almond flavoring	1 mL

Cheesecake (cont'd)

Combine whipping cream and sour cream. Beat in sugar. In microwave on low setting heat until just warm. Soften gelatin in water then dissolve over hot water. Add gelatin mixture to sour cream mixture.

Beat the cream cheese until soft; add flavorings. Gradually fold in whipping cream mixture. Pour into prepared pan. Refrigerate at least 4 hours.

Serve with fresh or frozen strawberries or raspberries or a choice of sauces.
SERVES: 12-15.

Strawberry Marshmallow Dessert

9" x 13"	crumb crust of choice	22 x 33 cm
4 cups	frozen strawberries, thawed and drained	1 L
1 cup	juice from strawberries and water to yield	250 mL
6 oz.	strawberry gelatin	170 g
2 cups	ice water	500 mL
1 lb.	marshmallows	500 g
1 cup	milk	250 mL
2 x 1½ oz.	pkgs. whipped topping, prepared	2 x 40 g

Heat juice and dissolve gelatin in it. Add ice water and chill until mixture starts to thicken. In microwave or double boiler melt marshmallows in milk. Cool and then blend in the whipped topping. Combine strawberries and gelatin mixture and fold into marshmallow mixture. Blend only until marble effect is reached. Pour over crust and chill until ready to serve.
SERVES: 6-8

Spumoni

2 cups	home-frozen unsweetened strawberries or raspberries, thawed and drained	500 mL
	OR	
15 oz.	pkg. commercially frozen strawberries or raspberries, thawed and drained	425 g
2 tbsp.	lemon juice	25 mL
3 tbsp.	sugar	50 mL
1 cup	chopped nuts	250 mL
½ cup	confectioner's icing sugar	125 mL
3 cups	whipping cream	750 mL

Mash the thawed berries. Add lemon juice and sugar and set aside for 30 minutes. Add the nuts and confectioner's icing sugar. Whip the cream and fold in the strawberry mixture. Pour into a loaf pan and freeze.

NOTE: If purchased berries are sweetened do not add the 3 tbsp. (50 mL) sugar.
SERVES: 6-8.

Snowstick Popsicles

8 oz.	cream cheese, softened	250 g
¼ cup	honey, liquid	50 mL
2 cups	home-frozen strawberries, thawed and drained, plus	500 mL
⅔ cup	juice from strawberries and water to yield	150 mL
	OR	
15 oz.	pkg. commercially frozen strawberries	425 g
3 cups	miniature marshmallows	750 mL
2 cups	whipped cream or whipped topping	500 mL

Snowstick Popsicles (cont'd)

Whip the cream cheese on low setting and gradually add the honey. Add strawberries and the juice. Fold in marshmallows and whipped cream. Spoon 5 ounces (125 mL) each into paper cups and insert sticks. Freeze 4 hours.

NOTE: If honey has solidified place measured amount in microwave on defrost to liquify.

Raspberries could be used in place of strawberries.
SERVES: 8.

Frozen Strawberry Yogurt Popsicles

3 cups	fresh strawberries, sliced	750 mL
	OR	
3 cups	thawed and drained frozen unsweetened strawberries	750 mL
½ cup	sugar	125 mL
1 cup	juice from strawberries and water to yield	250 mL
1 tbsp.	gelatin	15 mL
2 cups	yogurt	500 mL

For fresh strawberries: Combine strawberries and sugar and let stand at room temperature about 30 minutes. Drain strawberries and add water to yield 1 cup (250 mL).

For frozen strawberries: Thaw and drain 1 quart (1 L) package of strawberries. If more liquid is needed add water. Combine sugar with liquid.

Dissolve gelatin in liquid. Let stand about 5 minutes then slowly heat until gelatin is dissolved. Combine strawberries, gelatin liquid and yogurt in blender and purée to a smooth mixture. Pour 5 ounces (125 mL) each into paper cups. Insert wooden sticks and freeze overnight.

NOTE: Raspberries could be used in place of strawberries.
SERVES: 12.

Two Layers Are Better Than One

FIRST LAYER:

2 cups	milk	500 mL
3	egg yolks	3
1 cup	sugar	250 mL
½ tsp.	salt	2 mL
1¼ cup	whipping cream	300 mL
2 tsp.	vanilla	10 mL
½ tsp.	almond extract	2 mL
½ cup	chopped nuts	125 mL
few drops	green food coloring	few drops

SECOND LAYER:

2 cups	fresh strawberries	500 mL
	OR	
2 cups	frozen, unsweetened strawberries, thawed and drained	500 mL
¾ cup	sugar	175 mL
1 tsp.	lemon juice	5 mL
¼ tsp.	salt	1 mL
2	egg whites, beaten	2
1½ cups	whipping cream	375 mL

Scald milk. Beat the egg yolks, add sugar and salt and place in double boiler. Slowly add the milk to the egg mixture. Cook until mixture thickens. Cool. Add the cream (do not whip), flavorings and nuts. Tint pale green with food coloring. Pour into 9" x 13" (22 x 33 cm) pan. Place in quick-freeze area of freezer and freeze. Prepare second layer.

Combine strawberries and sugar and cook until strawberries are soft. Purée the mixture in a blender. Add lemon juice and salt. Beat egg whites to soft peaks and fold into purée. Whip the whipping cream and fold in. Pour over base and freeze.
SERVES: 12-15.

Banana Freeze With Strawberry Sauce

1 cup	mashed bananas (about 2 bananas)	250 mL
1 cup	applesauce	250 mL
⅓ cup	sugar	75 mL
⅛ tsp.	nutmeg	0.5 mL
⅛ tsp.	salt	0.5 mL
4 tsp.	lemon juice	20 mL
2 cups	whipped cream or whipped topping	500 mL

STRAWBERRY SAUCE:

4 cups	home-frozen sliced unsweetend strawberries, thawed and drained, plus	1 L
1½ cup	juice from berries and water to yield, plus	375 mL
½ cup	sugar OR	125 mL
2 x 10 oz.	pkgs. commercially frozen sliced sweetened strawberries, thawed and drained	2 x 283 g
1½ cups	juice from berries and water to yield	375 mL
1 tbsp.	cornstarch	15 mL
¼ tsp.	ginger	1 mL
2 tbsp.	chopped toasted almonds	25 mL

In a blender combine mashed banana, applesauce, sugar, nutmeg, salt and lemon juice. Blend until smooth. Empty into a bowl and fold in whipped cream. Pour into a loaf pan. Cover and freeze. Prepare sauce.

Combine the water and juice with cornstarch and ginger, (and sugar, if using home frozen strawberries). Cook and stir until thickened. Add strawberries and chill. At serving time slice the banana freeze and add strawberry sauce. Sprinkle with toasted almonds and serve.

SERVES: 8.

Strawberry Bombe

6 cups	vanilla ice cream, softened	1.5 L
1 tbsp.	gelatin	15 mL
¼ cup	cold water	50 mL
¼ cup	boiling water	50 mL
¼ tsp.	salt	1 mL
2	egg whites	2
½ cup	sugar	125 mL
1 tbsp.	lemon juice	15 mL
1 cup	whipping cream, whipped	250 mL
2 cups	home-frozen unsweetened sliced strawberries, drained, plus	500 mL
½ cup	juice from strawberries OR	125 mL
10 oz.	pkg. commercially frozen sliced strawberries	283 g

Line a 2½-quart (2.5 L) mixing bowl with aluminum foil. Line foil with the ice cream. Place in freezer until firm. Soften gelatin in cold water. Add boiling water. In small mixing bowl combine salt and egg whites and beat until foamy. Gradually add the sugar and continue beating until stiff. Add gelatin mixture and beat well. Let mixture stand until it begins to set, stirring occasionally. Add lemon juice to the whipped cream and carefully fold into egg white mixture. Fold in strawberries and juice to give a marble appearance. Pour into the frozen ice cream. Freeze overnight. At serving time unmold and decorate with icing. Use a confectioner's icing sugar recipe, tinted pale pink.
SERVES: 8-10.

BERRY QUICK
Combine 1 pkg. of prepared whipped topping, 1 quart (1 L) softened vanilla ice cream, 1 pint (500 mL) lime sherbet and ¼ cup (50 mL) creme de menthe. Freeze. Serve with strawberries or raspberries.

Frozen Berry Dessert

1 cup	flour, sifted	250 mL
¼ cup	brown sugar	50 mL
½ cup	chopped nuts	125 mL
½ cup	butter or margarine, melted	125 mL
2	egg whites	2
1 cup	sugar	250 mL
2 tbsp.	lemon juice	25 mL
2 cups	fresh strawberries or raspberries	500 mL
	OR	
2 cups	whole frozen strawberries or raspberries	500 mL
1 cup	whipping cream	250 mL

Preheat oven to 350°F (180°C).

Combine flour, sugar, nuts and butter. Pour mixture onto pizza pan or tray and bake 20 minutes. Stir frequently. Remove from oven and save ⅓ of crumb mixture for top. Spread remaining on bottom of 9" x 13" (22 x 33 cm) pan. Beat egg whites, sugar and lemon juice until stiff peaks form. Whip the cream. Fold whipped cream into egg whites. Fold strawberries or raspberries into mixture. Carefully pour over crumbs. Sprinkle top with remaining crumbs. Freeze 12 hours.
SERVES: 12-15.

Berry Ice

8 cups	strawberries or raspberries	2 L
1 tbsp.	orange juice	15 mL
2 cups	sugar	500 mL
4 cups	water	1 L

Purée fruit; add orange juice. Combine sugar and water and simmer 5 minutes. Add puréed fruit. Freeze. Mixture should be stirred several times before it freezes hard.
SERVES: 8.

Frozen Fruit Dessert Salad

Served on lettuce it can be a salad or without lettuce a dessert. Keep some in freezer to serve when unexpected company arrives or on hectic days when you need a little "something special".

14 oz.	pineapple, crushed, drained	398 mL
¼ cup	juice from pineapple to soften gelatin	50 mL
1 cup	remaining pineapple juice plus water to yield	250 mL
1 tbsp.	gelatin	15 mL
2 tbsp.	orange juice	25 mL
2 tbsp.	lemon juice	25 mL
2 cups	whipped cream or whipped topping	500 mL
2 cups	marshmallows, miniature	500 mL
¼ cup	mayonnaise	50 mL
1 cup	white grapes, fresh or canned, halved	250 mL
1 cup	diced peaches, fresh or canned	250 mL
3 cups	strawberries, fresh or whole frozen	750 mL
½ cup	chopped nuts	50 mL

Soften gelatin in ¼ cup (50 mL) of pineapple juice. Combine gelatin mixture and remaining pineapple juice plus water and warm slowly to dissolve gelatin. Add orange juice and lemon juice. Chill until mixture thickens. Fold in whipped cream, marshmallows, fruits and nuts. Spoon into containers leaving enough head space for expansion in freezing. Cover and freeze. Recipe will fill 4, 2-cup (500 mL) containers. Freeze in cottage cheese-type containers. Each 2-cup (500 g) container will serve 4-5. SERVES: 16-20.

Frozen Raspberry Dessert Salad

½ cup	boiling water	125 mL
6 oz.	raspberry gelatin	170 g
2 cups	home-frozen raspberries thawed and drained	500 mL
⅔ cup	juice from raspberries OR	150 mL
10 oz.	pkg. commercially frozen raspberries, thawed	283 g
6 oz.	cream cheese, softened	170 g
1 cup	sour cream	250 mL
14 oz.	whole cranberry sauce	398 mL
⅛ tsp.	salt	0.5 mL

Combine boiling water and gelatin. Add raspberries and juice. Add remaining ingredients and mix. Pour into 8" x 8" (20 x 20 cm) pan or into 3, 2-cup (500 mL) containers. Cover and freeze for 24 hours. Remove from freezer 10 minutes before serving. SERVES: 9-12.

Toasted Almond Shortcake

2 cups	flour, sifted	500 mL
1 tbsp.	baking powder	15 mL
1 tsp.	sugar	5 mL
½ tsp.	salt	2 mL
¼ cup	shortening	50 mL
¾ cup	milk	175 mL
3 tbsp.	butter, melted	50 mL
½ cup	toasted slivered almonds	125 mL

Preheat oven to 400°F (200°C).

Sift first 4 ingredients into medium-size bowl. Cut in shortening to make crumbs. Add milk, stir with fork until just moist. Knead a few times on lightly floured board. Divide dough in half. Pat each half into lightly greased 8" (20 cm) pan. Brush with melted butter; sprinkle with almonds. Lightly press almonds into dough. Bake about 30 minutes until golden brown. Break each cake into 6 pieces. Place 1 piece in individual dessert dish, add sweetened berries or sauces. Add another piece of shortcake and more berries or sauce.
SERVES: 6.

Summer Holiday Shortcake

4 cups	flour	1 L
8 tsp.	baking powder	40 mL
1 tsp.	cream of tartar	5 mL
1 tsp.	salt	5 mL
¼ cup	sugar	50 mL
1 cup	butter or margarine	250 mL
1⅓ cups	milk	325 mL

Preheat oven to 450°F (230°C).

Sift together flour, baking powder, cream of tartar, salt and sugar. Cut in butter. Add milk all at once. Stir in quickly. Turn onto flour-sprinkled board. Knead a few times. Pat into 9" x 13" (22 x 33 cm) pan. Bake about 20 minutes. Cool. Decorate with choice of Canadian or American designs (as follows).
SERVES: 12-15. See photograph page 80.

Canadian Shortcake

9" x 13"	shortcake (see above)	22 x 33 cm
2 cups	whipping cream	500 mL
8 cups	strawberries, halved	2 L

Place shortcake on serving tray. Whip the cream and sweeten to taste. Cover shortcake with whipped cream. Cover 1½" (4 cm) strips on left and right sides of shortcake with sliced straw-berries. Cut a maple leaf from stiff paper. (To make a pattern fold paper in half and make pattern 7" (18 cm) high). Have someone hold pattern over center of shortcake. Mark around pattern with toothpick. Fill in maple leaf with sliced or halved strawberries. Red raspberries could be used in place of straw-berries. Serve with additional berries and whipped cream if so desired.

American Shortcake

9" x 13"	shortcake, page 78	22 x 33 cm
2 cups	whipping cream	500 mL
2 cups	blueberries	500 mL
8 cups	strawberries, halved	2 L

Place shortcake on serving tray. Whip the cream and sweeten to taste. Cover shortcake with whipped cream. Measure a box 4½" (11 cm) deep by 5½" (14 cm) across in upper left hand corner. Fill in with blueberries. Make stripe number 1 across top of cake with strawberries. Make stripe number 4 keeping bottom of stripe parallel to bottom of blueberry box. Make stripe number 7 across bottom of shortcake. Fill in stripes 2 and 3 and 5 and 6. Serve with additional strawberries and whipped cream if desired. Raspberries could be used in place of strawberries.

Double Shortcake

⅓ cup	brown sugar	75 mL
1 tbsp.	grated orange peel	15 mL
3 cups	flour, sifted	750 mL
4 tsp.	baking powder	20 mL
1 tsp.	salt	5 mL
¾ cup	butter or margarine	175 mL
¾ cup	milk	175 mL
3 cups	ice cream of choice	750 mL
3 cups	strawberries or raspberries	750 mL

Preheat oven to 450°F (230°C).

Combine sugar and peel. Combine flour, baking powder and salt. Add ½ of brown sugar mixture. Cut in butter to resemble fine meal. Add milk, combine until just blended. Pat ½ of dough into greased round 9" (22 cm) pan. Drop remaining dough on an inverted round 8" (20 cm) pan. Make 8 equal mounds in a circle around outer edge of pan. Sprinkle tops with remaining brown sugar mixture. Bake 10-15 minutes. Spread ice cream over the 9" (22 cm) shortcake. Add layer of berries and top with circle of biscuits. Fill center with berries.
SERVES: 8.

Pan Shortcake

CAKE:

2	eggs, separated	2
1 cup	sugar	250 mL
⅓ cup	hot water	75 mL
¼ tsp.	lemon juice	1 mL
1 cup	cake flour, sifted	250 mL
1½ tsp.	baking powder	7 mL
¼ tsp.	salt	1 mL

FILLING:

4 cups	fresh sliced strawberries or raspberries	1 L
	OR	
4 cups	frozen strawberries or raspberries, thawed and drained	1 L
1 cup	juice from berries	250 mL
2 tbsp.	cornstarch	25 mL
½ tsp.	almond extract	2 mL

MERINGUE:

4	egg whites	4
½ tsp.	cream of tartar	2 mL
½ cup	sugar	125 mL

Preheat oven to 325°F (160°C).

Beat yolks until thick and lemon colored; gradually add ½ of sugar, water and lemon juice and beat. In another bowl beat egg whites until stiff but not dry. Gradually beat in remaining sugar. Fold egg whites into egg yolk mixture. Fold in the sifted dry ingredients. Pour batter into greased 9" x 13" (22 x 33 cm) pan. Bake about 35 minutes. Cool.

Cover the cake with fresh berries. If using frozen berries cook the juice and cornstarch until mixture thickens. Add almond extract and berries and spoon over cake. Preheat oven to 375°F (190°C). Prepare meringue.

Pan Shortcake (cont'd)

Beat egg whites with cream of tartar until soft peaks form. Gradually beat in sugar until stiff peaks form. Spread meringue over berries. Bake a few minutes until meringue is golden. SERVES: 12-15.

Strawberry Shortcake

A favorite recipe of dietitian Dorothy Kaack and family.

1 cup	miniature marshmallows	250 mL
4 cups	home-frozen strawberries, thawed and drained, plus	1 L
1 cup	strawberry juice, plus	250 mL
¼ cup	sugar	75 mL
	OR	
2 x 10 oz.	pkgs. commercially frozen sliced sweetened strawberries	2 x 283 g
3 oz.	strawberry gelatin	85 g
2¼ cups	flour, unsifted	550 mL
1½ cups	sugar	375 mL
½ cup	Crisco	125 mL
3 tsp.	baking powder	15 mL
½ tsp.	salt	2 mL
1 cup	milk	250 mL
1 tsp.	vanilla	5 mL
3	eggs	3

Preheat oven to 350°F (180°C).

Generously grease bottom only of a 9" x 13" (22 x 33 cm) pan. Sprinkle marshmallows evenly over bottom of pan. Combine thawed strawberries, juice and sugar if home frozen, or commercially frozen strawberries and syrup, with the dry strawberry gelatin; set aside. Place flour in large mixing bowl; add remaining ingredients, beat 3 minutes. Pour batter over marshmallows. Spoon strawberry mixture over batter. Bake 45-50 minutes. Serve warm or cool with ice cream or whipped cream. SERVES: 12-15.

Shortcake With Nuts

THE SHORTCAKE:

3 cups	flour	750 mL
½ cup	sugar	125 mL
1 tsp.	salt	5 mL
4 tsp.	baking powder	20 mL
½ tsp.	nutmeg	2 mL
½ tsp.	cinnamon	2 mL
½ tsp.	cardamom	2 mL
¾ cup	butter	175 mL
1 cup	finely chopped pecans or walnuts	250 mL
2	egg yolks	2
⅔ cup	milk	150 mL

THE FILLING:

4 cups	strawberries	1 L
¾ cup	sugar	175 mL
2	egg whites	2
1 cup	whipping cream	250 mL

Preheat oven to 450°F (230°C).

Sift flour, sugar, salt, baking powder and spices together. Rub butter into flour until it resembles fine bread crumbs. Add nuts. Beat egg yolks and milk together. Add to flour mixture. Knead a few times on lightly floured board. Divide dough into 3 pieces. Press each piece into 8" (20 cm) cake pan. Bake 12-15 minutes until golden brown. Turn out and cool on wire rack. Prepare filling.

Combine strawberries and sugar and set aside. Beat egg whites stiff. Whip the cream and fold into stiffly beaten egg whites. Divide strawberries and whipped cream mixture between layers and on top of shortcake.
SERVES: 6-8.

Muffin Shortcake

Recommended to strawberry growers by Ken Cybulsky of the Strawberry Patch at Selkirk, Manitoba.

THE BERRIES:

4 cups	strawberries or raspberries	1 L
¼ cup	honey	50 mL
1 tsp.	grated lemon peel	5 mL

THE SAUCE:

1 cup	sour cream	250 mL
3 tbsp.	honey	50 mL

THE SHORTCAKE:

1½ cups	flour, unsifted	375 mL
½ cup	sugar	125 mL
1 tbsp.	poppy seed	15 mL
2 tsp.	baking powder	10 mL
½ tsp.	salt	2 mL
¼ cup	shortening	50 mL
1	egg, beaten	1
¾ cup	milk	175 mL

Carefully combine berries, honey and peel and let stand while preparing the sauce and shortcake.

Stir together sour cream and honey until just blended.

Preheat oven to 400°F (200°C). Grease 12, 2½" x 1¼" (6.5 x 3 cm) muffin cups.

Combine flour, sugar, poppy seed, baking powder, and salt. Cut in shortening until mixture resembles coarse crumbs. Combine beaten egg and milk; add to flour mixture. Stir with fork until just moistened. Spoon into prepared muffin cups. Bake about 20 minutes. Split warm muffins, cover with berry mixture and top with sour cream mixture.

SERVES: 12.

Pizza Crust

1 cup	flour	250 mL
1 tbsp.	baking powder	15 mL
½ tsp.	salt	2 mL
2 tbsp.	vegetable oil	25 mL
½ cup	milk	125 mL

Preheat oven to 375°F (190°C).

Sift flour, baking powder and salt together. Combine vegetable oil and milk and add to dry ingredients. Knead about 20 times. Press into lightly oiled pizza pan. Cover with choice of toppings. Bake 15 to 20 minutes.

YIELDS: 12" (30 cm) pizza.

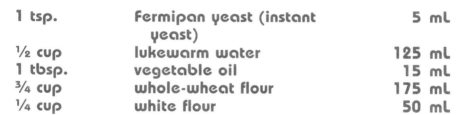

Whole-Wheat Pizza Crust

1 tsp.	Fermipan yeast (instant yeast)	5 mL
½ cup	lukewarm water	125 mL
1 tbsp.	vegetable oil	15 mL
¾ cup	whole-wheat flour	175 mL
¼ cup	white flour	50 mL

Preheat oven to 375°F (190°C).

In a medium-size bowl combine the yeast and lukewarm water. Add oil and whole-wheat and white flours. Knead until soft dough. Let rise 5 minutes. Spread on lightly oiled pizza pan. Cover with choice of toppings. Bake 15-20 minutes.

YIELDS: 12" (30 cm) pizza.

The kiwi fruit proves that beauty is more than skin deep.

Pizza Topping I

½ cup	frozen strawberries, thawed and drained, to yield	125 mL
½ cup	jellied cranberry sauce	125 mL
1 cup	shredded mozzarella cheese	250 mL

Preheat oven to 375°F (190°C).

Combine strawberries and cranberry sauce. Spread over pizza base. Sprinkle with shredded mozzarella cheese. Bake about 15-20 minutes.

Pizza Topping II

| 1 cup | strawberry jam | 250 mL |
| 1 cup | shredded Velveeta cheese | 250 mL |

Preheat oven to 375°F (190°C).

Spread pizza base with strawberry jam.

Sprinkle shredded Velveeta cheese on top. Bake about 15-20 minutes.

Pizza Topping III

1 cup	cottage cheese	250 mL
1 tbsp.	sour cream	15 mL
1	egg yolk	1
¾ cup	strawberry or raspberry jam	175 mL

Preheat oven to 375°F (190°C).

Combine cottage cheese, sour cream and egg yolk. Spread over pizza crust. Spread jam on top. Bake about 15-20 minutes.

Pizza Topping IV

1 cup	strawberry jam OR	250 mL
1 cup	raspberry jam	250 mL
1 tbsp.	grated crystallized ginger	15 mL
1 cup	shredded mozzarella cheese	250 mL
¾ cup	chopped nuts	175 mL

Preheat oven to 375°F (190°C).

Combine strawberry or raspberry jam and grated ginger. Spread over pizza crust. Sprinkle shredded mozzarella cheese over jam. Sprinkle nuts over the cheese. Bake about 15-20 minutes.

Dessert Pizza with Fresh Fruit

Requires about 1 ½ hours to prepare.

CRUST:

1½ tsp.	Fermipan yeast (instant yeast)	7 mL
½ cup	milk, warm	125 mL
2 tsp.	sugar	10 mL
½ tsp.	salt	2 mL
1 tbsp.	butter	15 mL
1	egg, slightly beaten	1
1⅓ cup	flour	325 mL

CHEESE TOPPING:

8 oz.	cream cheese	250 g
¼ cup	sugar	50 mL
1	egg yolk	1
1 tbsp.	grated ginger	15 mL
2 tbsp.	flour	25 mL
⅛ tsp.	cardamom	0.5 mL
⅛ tsp.	mace	0.5 mL

FRUIT TOPPING:

2 cups	strawberry halves	500 mL
2-3	bananas, sliced	2-3
4	kiwifruit, sliced	4
½ cup	currant jelly, melted	125 g

Dessert Pizza with Fresh Fruit (cont'd)

Add yeast to warm milk. Add sugar, salt, butter and beaten egg. Mix in flour. Knead 10 times. Grease a medium-size bowl. Add dough to bowl, turn dough to coat all surfaces. Cover with towel and let rise in warm area until double in volume, about 45 minutes. Press into 12" (31 cm) pizza pan.

Preheat oven to 350°F (180°C).

Beat cheese topping ingredients together. Spread over pizza crust. Bake about 20 minutes until browned and cheese topping is set. Cool. Decorate top with fruit. Brush with the melted jelly (raspberry or strawberry jelly may also be used). Serve.

NOTE: Other fruit combinations may be used.
SERVES: 8. See photograph page 64.

Cheese Tart

16 oz.	cream cheese, divided	500 g
½ cup	margarine	125 mL
1¼ cups	flour	300 mL
¼ tsp.	salt	1 mL
⅓ cup	sugar	75 mL
1 tbsp.	lemon juice	15 mL
1 cup	whipping cream	250 mL
	fresh fruit: strawberries, kiwifruit, nectarines	
¼ cup	apricot preserves	50 mL
1 tbsp.	water	15 mL

Preheat oven to 425°F (220°C).

Combine 4 oz. (125 g) cream cheese and margarine. Mix until well blended. Add flour and salt and form into a ball. Chill. On lightly floured surface roll out dough to fit 12" (30 cm) tart or pizza pan. Prick bottom and sides with fork. Bake 12-15 minutes. Cool. Combine remaining cream cheese, sugar and lemon juice and mix. Whip the cream and fold in. Spoon onto crust. Arrange fruit on top. Brush with mixture of apricot preserves and water.
SERVES: 10.

Sweet Strawberry Pizza*

1 loaf	frozen white bread dough, thawed and cut in half crosswise	500 g
16 oz.	cream cheese	500 g
½ cup	sugar	125 mL
6 tbsp.	flour	75 mL
2	egg yolks	2
2 tsp.	fresh lemon juice	10 mL
1 tsp.	grated lemon peel	5 mL
⅓ cup	homemade strawberry jam, divided	150 mL
2 tbsp.	sliced toasted almonds	25 mL
2 cups	halved fresh strawberries	500 mL

Place each half of dough on greased baking sheet or pizza pan. Cover with greased foil and towel and let rise until double. Pat each half into 12" (30 cm) circle, each about ¼" (0.6 cm) thick. In mixing bowl place cream cheese, sugar, flour, egg yolks, lemon juice and peel and beat until smooth. Spread each circle of dough with half the cheese mixture to within ½" (1.3 cm) of edge. Cover loosely with greased foil and a towel; let rise 45 minutes.

Bake in preheated oven 375°F (190°C) oven for 20 to 25 minutes, until lightly browned. Remove from oven and spread each pizza with strawberry jam; sprinkle with almonds. Bake 5 minutes longer. Serve hot.

For extra flavor place halved fresh strawberries on hot jam topping and serve. Leftover pizza wedges are good toasted in a toaster oven.

YIELDS: 2, 12" (30 cm) pizzas.

88

Meringues
Pies
Tarts
Jams

Basic Meringue

4	egg whites, room temperature	4
¼ tsp.	cream of tartar	1 mL
¼ tsp.	salt	1 mL
1 cup	sugar	250 mL
¼ tsp.	almond extract	1 mL

Preheat oven to 275°F (140°C).

Beat egg white with cream of tartar and salt until stiff but not dry. Add sugar gradually, about 1 tbsp. (15 mL) at a time, beating well after each addition, until all sugar is used and meringue is stiff. Grease and lightly flour trays or pie plate.

Bake as instructed in following recipes.

YIELDS: 48, 2" (5 cm) shallow meringues
12, 3" (8 cm) meringues
3, 8" (20 cm) circles
1, 10" (25 cm) shell in pie plate

Meringue Torte

MERINGUE:

Have ready 3, 8" (20 cm) meringue circles (When preparing the circles make the surface smooth.) Use Basic Meringue recipe for meringues.

Bake at 275°F (140°C) for 1 hour. Cool.

FILLING:

4 cups	raspberry sherbet	1 L
2 cups	whipping cream	500 mL
2 tbsp.	blackberry-flavored brandy	25 mL
2 tbsp.	raspberry preserves	25 mL

Meringue Torte (cont'd)

BERRY SAUCE:

2 cups	home-frozen raspberries, thawed	500 mL
	OR	
15 oz.	pkg. commercially frozen raspberries, thawed	425 g
2 cups	strawberries, halved	500 mL
3 tbsp.	blackberry-flavored brandy	50 mL

Line an 8" (20 cm) layer cake pan with foil. Spread sherbet in pan to make a smooth layer. Cover and freeze at least 2 hours.

In small bowl whip 1 cup (250 mL) of whipping cream until softly mounded. Add blackberry brandy and raspberry preserves and whip until stiff.

Place 1 meringue layer on flat tray. Unwrap sherbet and use as next layer. Add second meringue. Cover with blackberry-whipped cream. Add third meringue.

Whip remaining 1 cup (250 mL) whipping cream until stiff. Cover sides of torte with whipped cream. Use pastry bag to decorate top with whipped cream.

Freeze until firm, then wrap and return to freezer.

Before serving time prepare Berry Sauce. Heat raspberries to boiling. Press through sieve to remove seeds. Cool. Add sliced strawberries and blackberry brandy and combine. If unsweetened raspberries are used add sugar to taste.

At serving time remove torte from freezer. Place on serving tray. Cut with sharp knife and serve with Berry Sauce.

SERVES: 8-10.

Angel Pie

MERINGUE:

Use basic meringue recipe. Spread into a well-buttered 10" (25 cm) pie plate. Bake 1 hour at 275°F (140°C). Cool.

FILLING:

4	egg yolks	4
½ cup	sugar	125 mL
3 tbsp.	lime juice	50 mL
2 tbsp.	grated lime rind	25 mL
¼ tsp.	salt	1 mL
1 cup	whipping cream, whipped	250 mL
1½ cups	fresh strawberries	375 mL
	OR	
1½ cups	whole frozen strawberries, partly thawed	375 mL

Beat egg yolks until thick. Add next 4 ingredients. Cook in double boiler until thick. Cool. Fold in prepared whipped cream. Carefully pour into meringue shell. Chill 6 hours. At serving time add the strawberries or raspberries if you wish.

SERVES: 8.

Meringue Delights

MERINGUES:

Use basic meringue recipe. Grease and flour trays. Drop from teaspoon or use pastry bag to make 2" (5 cm) meringues. Use a spoon to build up sides of meringues. Bake 50 minutes at 275°F (140°C). Cool.

FILLING:

1 cup	semisweet chocolate chips	250 mL
¼ cup	butter or margarine	50 mL
4	egg yolks, slightly beaten	4
2 tbsp.	corn syrup	25 mL
48	strawberries, hulled	48

Meringue Delights (cont'd)

Combine chocolate morsels and butter and melt over hot water. Combine egg yolks and corn syrup, add to chocolate mixture. Cook and stir 5 minutes. Remove from heat and beat until mixture is of spreading consistency. Place about ½ tsp. (2 mL) chocolate mixture in each meringue. Top with 1 whole strawberry, stem end down, in chocolate mixture.

YIELDS: 48. See photograph page 32.

Magnificent Meringue

1 cup	egg whites, room temperature	250 mL
2 cups	fine berry sugar	500 mL
3 cups	whipping cream	750 mL
3 cups	strawberries, fresh, caps on	750 mL
3	kiwifruit, sliced, optional	3

Preheat oven to 200°F (95°C).

Beat the egg whites stiff; gradually add sugar about 2 tbsp. (25 mL) at a time. Continue beating until all the sugar is used. Drop mixture onto buttered baking sheets using a tablespoon or pastry bag. Bake 2 hours or until the meringues are dry. Cool.

Whip the cream. Using a pastry bag put dabs of whipped cream on serving tray to secure first layer of meringues. Use additional rosettes of whipped cream and remaining meringues to build a pyramid or dome-shaped cake. Refrigerate 1 hour. Garnish with strawberries and sliced kiwifruit, if used.

SERVES: 12-15. See photograph on cover.

Sublime Meringue Torte

6	egg whites	6
1¾ cups	sugar	425 mL
1 tsp.	vanilla	5 mL
1 tsp.	vinegar	5 mL

FILLING:

8 oz.	cream cheese, softened	250 g
1 cup	sugar	250 mL
1 tsp.	vanilla	5 mL
1 cup	whipping cream	250 mL
2 cups	miniature marshmallows	500 mL

TOPPING:

2 cups	frozen sliced strawberries, or whole medium-sized strawberries, thawed	500 mL
1 tsp.	lemon juice	5 mL
19 oz.	cherry pie filling	540 mL

Preheat oven to 275°F (140°C).

Beat egg whites until stiff enough to hold peaks. Beat in sugar about 2 tbsp. (25 mL) at a time. Add vanilla and vinegar. Grease and flour a 10" (25 cm) springform pan. Carefully pour meringue into pan. Use back of spoon to build up sides. Bake about 1 hour. Cool.

To prepare filling, whip cream cheese, sugar and vanilla. Whip the cream and fold in. Fold in marshmallows. Gently spoon filling into center of cooled meringue. Refrigerate 12 hours or overnight.

Combine topping ingredients. At serving time cut torte into wedges. Spoon topping on each serving.

BERRY QUICK FROSTED STRAWBERRIES:
Dip fresh strawberries with caps on into beaten egg white and then into sugar. Let dry.

Berry Meringues

MERINGUES:

Use basic Meringue recipe. Grease and flour trays. Drop from spoon or use pastry bag to make 12, 3" (8 cm) meringues. Use a spoon to build up sides of meringues. Bake 50 minutes at 275°F (140°C). Cool.

BERRY GLAZE:

1 cup	strawberries or raspberries	250 mL
1 cup	water	250 mL
¾ cup	sugar	175 mL
3 tbsp.	cornstarch	50 mL

FILLING:

3-4 cups	strawberries or raspberries	750 mL- 1 L

TOPPING:

½ cup	sour cream	125 mL
2 tbsp.	milk	25 mL
½ cup	brown sugar	125 mL

Prepare Berry Glaze. Crush the berries. Add the water. Bring to a boil and simmer 2 minutes. Sieve to remove seeds. Combine sieved mixture, sugar and cornstarch. Cook and stir over medium heat until mixture thickens.

Place strawberries or raspberries in meringues. Cover with berry glaze. Refrigerate at least 2 hours. At serving time add topping made by combining sour cream and milk. Drizzle over top of berry glaze. Sprinkle brown sugar on top.
SERVES: 12.

BERRY QUICK FROSTED STRAWBERRIES:
Dip whole frozen strawberries into liquid flavored gelatin mixture. Freeze.

Chocolate Filling For Meringues

6 oz.	semisweet chocolate	170 g
1 tbsp.	brandy	15 mL
1 cup	whipping cream	250 mL
1 tsp.	vanilla	5 mL

Melt chocolate with brandy. Cool. Whip the cream, add vanilla. To fill meringues, spoon in chocolate mixture, add some whipped cream and top with fresh or defrosted frozen strawberries or raspberries.

YIELDS: Filling for 12, 3" (8 cm) meringues.

Berry Ice Cream Pie

9"	baked pastry crust	22 cm
1 cup	fresh strawberies or raspberries	250 mL
	OR	
1 cup	frozen unsweetened strawberries or raspberries, thawed and drained	250 mL
3 tbsp.	sugar	50 mL
¼ tsp.	salt	1 mL
2	egg whites	2
¼ cup	sugar	50 mL
½ cup	marshmallow sundae topping	125 mL
1 qt.	vanilla ice cream	1 L

Add the 3 tbsp. (50 mL) sugar to the berries and set aside. Fresh berries should be slightly crushed. Combine salt and egg whites and beat until foamy. Slowly add sugar and beat until soft peak stage. Fold in the marshmallow sundae topping. Carefully fill pastry shell with ice cream. Cover ice cream with the strawberries or raspberries. Swirl the marshmallow meringue on top. Brown under broiler about 1 minute or until lightly browned. Serve immediately.

Easy Strawberry Pie

10"	baked crust	25 cm
3 cups	frozen strawberries, thawed and drained	750 mL
1 cup	juice from strawberries and water to yield	250 mL
3 oz.	strawberry gelatin	85 g
2 cups	vanilla ice cream	500 mL

Dissolve the gelatin in the 1 cup (250 mL) of juice heated to boiling. Add the ice cream and strawberries and mix. Pour into shell. Chill until firm.

This could be made with raspberries and raspberry gelatin.

Fresh Strawberry or Raspberry Sour Cream Pie

9"	unbaked pastry shell	22 cm
4 cups	strawberries, halved or raspberries	1 L
1¼ cups	sugar	300 mL
1 cup	flour	250 mL
¼ tsp.	salt	1 mL
1 cup	sour cream	250 mL
2 tbsp.	sugar	25 mL

Preheat oven to 450°F (230°C).

Place berries in shell. Sift together sugar, flour and salt and fold into sour cream. Pour over berries. Sprinkle top with sugar. Bake at 450°F (230°C) for 10 minutes, then 350°F (180°C) for about 30 minutes or until lightly browned.

We also prepared this with frozen berries that had been thawed and well drained.
SERVES: 6.

Strawberry Pie — Whitmer Style

This is a favorite of the Whitmer family of Ohio. It was a large family so has been well tested. Thanks to Jeannette Whitmer Eaton who now lives in California with husband Don.

9"	baked pastry shell	22 cm	
1	recipe of 7-minute frosting	1	
4 cups	strawberries	1 L	
3	strawberries with caps	3	

Spread half of frosting in pastry shell. Fill with berries. Add remaining frosting and garnish with the 3 strawberries.
SERVES: 6.

Fresh Strawberry Pie

A favorite of Epp's Berry Ranch at Saskatoon

9"	baked pastry or crust shell	22 cm	
3 oz.	cream cheese, softened	85 g	
3 tbsp.	milk	50 mL	
2 cups	strawberries, divided	500 mL	
½ cup	sugar	125 mL	
⅛ tsp.	salt	0.5 mL	
¼ cup	water	50 mL	
¼ cup	cornstarch	50 mL	
¼ cup	water	50 mL	
1 tbsp.	lemon juice	15 mL	

Beat cream cheese and milk together. Spread over bottom of crust. Prepare glaze: place 1 cup (250 mL) of strawberries in saucepan with the sugar, salt and ¼ cup (50 mL) water. Bring to a boil and cook and stir for 3 minutes. Combine the cornstarch and the remaining ¼ cup (50 mL) water, add to glaze mixture and cook and stir until thick. Add lemon juice.

Spread ½ of glaze on the cream cheese. Place the remaining 1 cup (250 mL) of berries with stem ends down on top of glaze. Spoon remaining glaze over top of berries.
SERVES: 6.

Raspberry Pie Deluxe

10"	baked pastry shell	25 cm
3 oz.	raspberry gelatin	85 g
½ cup	boiling water	125 mL
1 cup	home-frozen raspberries, thawed and drained, plus	250 mL
⅓ cup	juice from berries	150 mL
	OR	
10 oz.	pkg. commercially frozen raspberries	283 g
1 tbsp.	gelatin	15 mL
¼ cup	cold water	50 mL
3¼ oz.	pkg. vanilla pudding (regular type)	113 g
1¾ cup	milk	425 mL
1 tsp.	almond flavoring	5 mL
½ cup	sugar	125 mL
3	egg whites, beaten stiff	3
2 cups	whipped cream or whipped topping	500 mL
¼ cup	chopped nuts	50 mL

Dissolve raspberry gelatin in boiling water. Add raspberries and juice. Chill over ice water until partly thickened. Pour into pie shell and chill.

Soften gelatin in cold water. Prepare pudding using 1¾ cups (425 mL) milk. Add the gelatin mixture and stir until dissolved; add almond flavoring. Cool until partly set then beat until smooth.

Gradually beat sugar into egg whites. Fold into pudding with 1 cup (250 mL) whipped cream. Carefully spoon mixture over raspberry layer. Cool.

Before serving decorate top with remaining 1 cup (250 mL) of whipped cream. Sprinkle with nuts.

It takes some time but is worth every minute!
SERVES: 6-8.

Strawberry
Mom's ~~Apple~~ Pie

Mom used this recipe for many years. My first experience was a disaster as the pie slipped when I cut into it with a fork. It went from the table to the wall and onto the carpet.

A number of years later I started using the never-fail pastry which follows.

9"	baked pastry shell	22 cm
1¼ cups	cold water	300 mL
1⅓ cups	sugar	325 mL
¼ cup	cornstarch	50 mL
1 tbsp.	lemon juice	15 mL
4 cups	strawberries	1 L
few drops	red food coloring, optional	few drops
1 cup	whipped cream or whipped topping	250 mL

Combine ¾ cup (175 mL) of the water with sugar. Bring to a boil. Combine the remaining ½ cup water with cornstarch and blend. Slowly add to the sugar water mixture. Cook and stir until thick. Remove from heat; add lemon juice. Cool. Arrange berries in pie shell. Spoon sauce over top. Before serving decorate top with swirls of whipped cream and fresh strawberries with caps on.

SERVES: 6.

Never-Fail Pastry

5 cups	flour	1.25 L
1 tbsp.	salt	15 mL
1 lb.	lard	500 g
1 tbsp.	vinegar	15 mL
1	egg	1
	cold water	

Never-Fail Pastry (cont'd)

In mixing bowl combine flour and salt. Cut in lard until mixture resembles coarse crumbs. Measure 1 tbsp. (15 mL) of vinegar into measuring cup; add the egg and mix with fork. Add water to measure 1 cup (250 mL). Add liquid to flour mixture and mix. Press into a ball. Dough may be stored in refrigerator or in freezer. Roll out and use as needed. Prick crust all over with a fork if baking empty. Bake at 400°F (200°C) for 10-15 minutes. YIELDS: 6 pie shells or 3 double-crust pies.

Grower's Choice Pie

A choice selection of Berry Hill Farm at Altona, Manitoba and Epp's Berry Ranch at Saskatoon, Saskatchewan.

10"	crust of choice	25 cm
1 cup	thawed, drained frozen strawberries or raspberries	250 mL
1 cup	sugar	250 mL
2	egg whites	2
1 tbsp.	lemon juice	15 mL
⅛ tsp.	salt	0.5 mL
½ cup	whipping cream	125 mL
1 tsp.	vanilla	5 mL

In LARGE mixing bowl combine berries, sugar, egg whites, lemon juice and salt. Beat at least <u>15</u> minutes to create a fluffy mixture. In small bowl whip the cream; add vanilla. Fold whipped cream into berry mixture. Pile into prepared crust. Freeze. This pie should be removed from freezer just before serving.
SERVES: 6-8.

 BERRY QUICK RED, WHITE AND BLUE PARFAIT:
Combine prepared vanilla pudding, blueberries and strawberries or raspberries.

Rice Krispie Tarts

2 tbsp.	butter or margarine	25 mL
20	marshmallows, large	20
2½ cups	rice krispies	625 mL

FILLING:

2 cups	whipped cream	500 mL
1 cup	home-frozen strawberries or raspberries, thawed and drained	250 mL
	OR	
15 oz.	pkg. commercially-frozen strawberries or raspberries, thawed and drained	425 g

Melt butter or margarine over heat; add marshmallows. Cook while continually stirring until smooth. Remove from heat. Add rice krispies and mix. Butter 12 muffin tins, 2¾" (7 cm) size. Use about 1 heaping tablespoon (20 mL) of mixture per muffin cup. Press into cups to form shells.

For the filling combine the whipped cream and the strawberries or raspberries. Remove shells from muffin pans and fill with the combined whipped cream and fruit.
SERVES: 12.

Berry Quick Tarts:

Keep a supply of baked tart shells in freezer!

DEVONSHIRE TARTS:
Beat 3 ounces (85 g) cream cheese with ⅓ cup (75 mL) heavy cream until smooth. Spread layer in baked tart shells. Add layer of strawberries or raspberries. Glaze with melted currant jelly.

MARG OLSON'S TARTS:
Spread baked tart shells with commercial pineapple-cream cheese mixture. Fill with strawberries and glaze with melted wild cranberry jelly or currant jelly. Jelly can be heated with a little water to make the glaze.

Cooked Raspberry or Strawberry Jelly

4 cups	prepared raspberry juice (crush 10 cups [2.5 L] berries and place in jelly bag)	1 L
7½ cups	sugar	1875 mL
1	bottle liquid pectin	1

Measure juice into saucepan; add sugar and mix. Bring to a boil while stirring constantly. Add liquid pectin and bring to a full rolling boil for 1 minute. Remove from heat and skim off foam. Pour into glasses and seal.

For Strawberry Jelly Use:

3¾ cups	strawberry juice	925 mL
¼ cup	lemon juice	50 mL

Proceed as directions for raspberry jelly.
YIELDS: 11 medium glasses

Freezer Strawberry Jam

2 cups	crushed strawberries	500 mL
4 cups	sugar	1 L
2 oz.	pkg. pectin crystals	57 g
¾ cup	water	175 mL

Combine crushed strawberries and sugar and mix thoroughly. Let stand 10-15 minutes. In small saucepan combine pectin crystals and water. Bring to a boil and cook and stir for 1 minute. Combine with fruit mixture and stir at least **three** minutes. Ladle into containers and cover tightly with lids. Let stand at room temperature. 24 hours. Store in freezer.
YIELDS: 4½ cups (1.1 L)

BERRY QUICK BERRY TARTS:
Combine 1 cup (250 mL) fresh strawberries or rasp-berries, ½ cup (125 mL) sour cream or whipped cream and 2 tbsp. (25 mL) brown sugar. Spoon into baked tart shells.

Grandma's Strawberry Jam*

4 cups	strawberries	1 L
4 cups	sugar	1 L
½ cup	lemon juice	125 mL

Wash and hull strawberries. Place the strawberries into a casserole dish. Gently mix in the sugar. Cover and let stand at room temperature overnight. In the morning, stir mixture gently, then pour into a heavy saucepan. Bring to a rolling boil, stirring gently once or twice. Boil 8 minutes. Add the lemon juice. Boil another 3 minutes. Remove from heat. Skim with metal spoon. Let stand until cool. Pour into sterilized jars. Seal with paraffin.
YIELDS: 4 cups (1 L).

Certo Light Strawberry or Raspberry Jam

6 cups	strawberries, crushed	1400 mL
4½ cups	sugar	1050 mL
1¾ oz.	pkg. Certo Light pectin crystals	49 g

Place the crushed strawberries in a large saucepan. In a small bowl mix ¼ cup (50 mL) of sugar with Certo Light crystals. Slowly add Certo Light mixture to prepared fruit. On high heat cook and stir until mixture comes to full boil. Stir in remaining sugar. Cook and stir until mixture returns to full boil and then continue boiling and stirring for 1 minute. Remove from heat; skim off foam with metal spoon. Pour into sterilized jars filling to ⅛" (.3 cm) from the top. Cover immediately with lids and screw bands. Process in boiling water bath for 10 minute.

For raspberry jam use 6 cups (1400 mL) crushed raspberries in place of strawberries.
YIELDS: 6-8 cups.

Sugarless Strawberry or Raspberry Jam

1 tbsp.	gelatin	15 mL
2 cups	crushed strawberries or raspberries	500 mL
1 tbsp.	lemon juice	15 mL
1½-2 tbsp.	liquid artificial sweetener	20-25 mL

Soften gelatin in ½ cup (125 mL) of the crushed strawberries. After 5 minutes dissolve over hot water. Combine gelatin mixture, strawberries, lemon juice and desired amount of liquid artificial sweetener and mix well. Pour into prepared jars and seal. This jam must be refrigerated and will keep up to 6 weeks. YIELDS: 2 cups (500 mL).

Freezer Raspberry Jam

3 cups	crushed raspberries	750 mL
5¼ cups	sugar	1.4 L
2 oz.	pkg. pectin crystals	57 g
¾ cup	water	175 mL

One-half of raspberry pulp may be sieved to remove seeds if desired. Add sugar to crushed raspberries and mix thoroughly. Let stand 10-15 minutes. In small saucepan combine pectin crystals and water. Bring to a boil and cook and stir for 1 minute. Combine with fruit mixture and stir at least **three** minutes. Ladle into containers and cover tightly with lids. Let stand at room temperature 24 hours. Store in freezer. YIELDS: 4½ cups (1.1 L)

Jars of homemade strawberry or raspberry jams and jellies are thoughtful gifts.

Special Acknowledgements To:

Manitoba Agriculture and Strawberry Growers' Association for use of recipes marked with an asterisk.* *Recipes tested by staff of the Marketing Branch, Manitoba Agriculture and contributed through the courtesy of the Strawberry Growers' Association of Manitoba.

Peter J. Peters for the information on the development of the U-pick system and the Ode To the Strawberry.

Cheryl Odgers for her expert assistance in testing and adapting recipes. The recipes were further tested on her family and they found fruit soup and strawberry pizza most acceptable.

Emily Bennett for proofreading and "giving back" strawberries for recipe testing.

All friends, relatives and growers for the recipes and the encouragement in writing the book.

Jean Nilsson Noethlich, my niece, for the outstanding artwork.

My husband Alex and my daughter Ann for caring and sharing in all phases of this book.

Index

A Beautiful Gift For All Seasons

Berries Beautiful!

Please send _____ copies of Berries Beautiful at $8.95 each, plus $1.50 (total orders) for postage and handling to:

NAME: _____

STREET: _____

CITY: _____

PROVINCE/STATE: _____ POSTAL CODE/ZIP: _____

Make cheque or money order payable to:

American orders — please pay in U.S. funds

Carol Olson Publishing
P.O. Box 3
Spy Hill, Saskatchewan
Canada   S0A 3W0

A Beautiful Gift For All Seasons

Berries Beautiful!

Please send _____ copies of Berries Beautiful at $8.95 each, plus $1.50 (total orders) for postage and handling to:

NAME: _____

STREET: _____

CITY: _____

PROVINCE/STATE: _____ POSTAL CODE/ZIP: _____

Make cheque or money order payable to:

American orders — please pay in U.S. funds

Carol Olson Publishing
P.O. Box 3
Spy Hill, Saskatchewan
Canada   S0A 3W0